# 1 MONTH OF
# FREE
# READING

## at
## www.ForgottenBooks.com

By purchasing this book you are eligible for one month membership to ForgottenBooks.com, giving you unlimited access to our entire collection of over 1,000,000 titles via our web site and mobile apps.

To claim your free month visit: www.forgottenbooks.com/free888947

ISBN 978-0-266-78488-3
PIBN 10888947

This book is a reproduction of an important historical work. Forgotten Books uses
state-of-the-art technology to digitally reconstruct the work, preserving the original format
whilst repairing imperfections present in the aged copy. In rare cases, an imperfection in
the original, such as a blemish or missing page, may be replicated in our edition. We do,
however, repair the vast majority of imperfections successfully; any imperfections that
remain are intentionally left to preserve the state of such historical works.

# REPORTS FROM COUNTIES.

## COUNTY ANTRIM.

### Ballykeel Churchyard—Islandmagee.

[From Mr. W. F. Reynolds.]

'An old graveyard lies in what is locally called "The Slack of the Island," in the townland of Ballykeel, about one half mile, north-west, from the foot of Muldersley Hill, and the same distance, east, from the Ballycarry Station of the Northern Railway, running from Belfast to Larne, on the opposite shore of Larne Lough.

'This graveyard is a very small one, and contains the ivy-covered, ruined walls of an old rectangular church, about 60 feet long by 24 feet wide. Many interments have taken place in the enclosed area, access to which is had by means of a few rough stone steps built at the lowest point in the southern wall. The grave-stones, all of which are upright, are numerous, relative to the size of the place; their inscriptions may be read without much trouble, having doubtless been preserved owing to the sheltered position of the burying-ground; many stones also have been cleaned or painted, and a few of them have had their lettering renewed':—

> Sacred to the memory of Thomas Hill, formerly School-master of Islandmagee, who died 24th March 1821 aged 62 years.
> His kind attention to his scholars & benevolence to all is the cause of this stone being erected.

> Here lieth the body of James Hill who deceased 13th February 1816 aged 88 years. Also his wife, Jane Hill, otherwise Brennan, who deceased 14th January 1818, aged 83 years.
> These lines by Samuel Broadford in memory of his aunt Serra Hill who died on the 24th of April 1850, aged 84 years.

'Above inscription is cut on the back of the stone; on the front, on either side of, and below a coat-of-arms, the following inscription appears ' : —

Here     Lyeth
y̆ Body     of Isab
el Mᶜel    wen who
died Ja     nuary

y̆ 22 1746. Aged 43 years.

Sacred to the memory of Thomas Colville who died 17ᵗʰ September 1840 aged 86 years. His wife, Mary Milliken died 17ᵗʰ Nov 1850 aged 86 years. Their son, James, was lost at sea, May 1808, aged 19 years : their son, Thomas, died 6ᵗʰ Janʸ 1875 aged 74 years.

———

Erected by Richard Thompson, of Belfast, to the memory of William Thompson who departed this life 20ᵗʰ July 1813 aged 90 years. Also his wife, Margᵗ Thompson who departed this life 12ᵗʰ January 1778 aged 47 years.

———

Here lyeth the body of Mʳ William Hill who died Sepᵇʳ yᵉ 24ᵗʰ 1734 aged 54 years.
Here also lyeth yᵉ body of his wife Elezᵗʰ Hill who died Ianʳʸ yᵉ 7ᵗʰ 1752, aged 52 years.

———

Here lyeth the body of James Hill who departed this life July yᵉ 13ᵗʰ 1733, aged 62 years. Also Jean Hill, his wife, who departed this life February the 12ᵗʰ 1751, aged 72 years.

Here lieth the body of John Brackenridge who departed
this life January 2<sup>nd</sup> 1763 aged 63 years.   Likewise his
wife, Agnes Brackenridge, who departed this life Jan<sup>ry</sup>
14<sup>th</sup> 1794 aged 73 years.

Erected by To<sup>s</sup> Hill to the memory of his father, Wil<sup>m</sup>
Hill who departed this life the 13<sup>th</sup> of April 1821 aged
61 years.   Also his wife, Sarah Nelson, who departed
this life the 1<sup>st</sup> of April 1817 aged 48 years

Erected by Robert Wilson, of Belfast, in memory of his
beloved wife, Margaret Hill, who departed this life 24<sup>th</sup>
July 1744 aged 40 years.   Also their eldest son, Robert,
who was drowned from on board the ship " Amoy," of
Belfast, in Quebec River on the 11<sup>th</sup> August 1845 aged
16 years.

Erected by William Hill of Islandmagee to the memory
of his wife, Mary Boyle, who deceased the 24<sup>th</sup> of March
1807 aged 41 years.   Also their son, Samuel, who de-
ceased the 3<sup>rd</sup> Feb<sup>y</sup> 1797 aged 8 days.   Also the said
William Hill who departed this life on the 12<sup>th</sup> of June
1847 aged 90 years.

' The foregoing are all inside the old building.'

' On the outer side of the eastern gable six mural tablets stand,
ide by side, bearing inscriptions referring to the name Nelson :—

Here lyeth the body of Gilbart Nilson who departed this
life January the 13<sup>th</sup> 1720 aged 59 years.   Also his son,
Thomas, who died Janury y<sup>e</sup> 14, 1787 aged 62.   J. N.
who departed this life Agust y<sup>e</sup>—2<sup>th</sup> 17— aged 72 years.

Erected in memory of Robert Nelson who departed this
life Nove<sup>r</sup> the 20<sup>th</sup> 1814 aged 6 years.   Also Margaret
Nilson who departed this life December 2<sup>nd</sup> 1815 aged
3 years.   Also Andrew Nelson, their father, who died
Feb<sup>y</sup> 25<sup>th</sup> 1856, aged 79 years.   Marg<sup>t</sup> Nelson, his wife,
died 2<sup>nd</sup> Aug 1859 Æ 77 years.

—ere lieth the body — Agness Holmes other — is—
Nilson wife to John Nilson — depart— this life — —h
—20<sup>th</sup> of April 1789 — d 33 years.   Also 2 of—
—hildren, Jennet & Mary.   Also Mary Faires otherwise
Nilson wife to the said John Nil— —ho deceased 15<sup>th</sup>
Dec<sup>r</sup> 1817 aged 57 years.   Also the above named John
Nilson who departed this life 15<sup>th</sup> February 1821 aged
60 years.

Here lieth the body of Gilbert Nelson who dep[d] this life the 3rd day of December 1774 aged 64 years. Also Jannet Rea who departed this life 19th Nov[r] 1791 aged 53 years. Also her husband, Thomas Nilson who departed this life the 16th of August 1815 aged 84 years.

---

Thomas Nelson in memory of his wife, Mary Nelson, who departed this life 20th January 1856 aged 39 years. Also his son, William, who died 11th January 1849 aged 7 months. Also the above Thomas Nelson died 23rd October 1858 aged 40 years.

---

Erected by William & Jenny Gray in memory of her brother, William Nelson who died 27th July 1839 aged 5 years : her mother, Jenny Nelson, who died 31st Dec[r] 1861 aged 60 years : her father John Nelson who died 4th April 1875 aged 78 years.

---

' In the yard, around ruins, are to be found the following ' :—

Here lyeth ye body of John Brynan who departed this life y[e] 9th of December 1729 aged 70 years.

---

Erected by William Adam in memory of his mother, Isabella Lemmon who died 5th December 1821 aged 37 years.

---

Here lyeth the body of Robert Brynan who departed this life April 3rd 1802 aged 73 years. Also Margaret Brynnan, his wife, who departed this life the 16th of October 1807 aged 78 years. Also his son, Henry Brenan, who departed this life 14th Feb[y] 1845 aged 88 years and of John Brenan, his son, who departed this life in Feb[y] 1837 aged 78 years. Also Henery Brenan died the 3rd of June 1847 aged 54 years. Also Robert Brenan died the 21st of September 1851 aged 87 years.

---

Erected in memory of Randal M[c]Murtry who died 6th April 1862 aged 79 years : also his wife Jenny who died 15th January 1878 aged 88 years.

Here lieth the body of the Rev<sup>d</sup> James M<sup>c</sup>Cauley who
departed this life the 10<sup>th</sup> of August 1822 aged 81 y<sup>rs.</sup>
Also his daughter, Jane M<sup>c</sup>Cauley, who died 17<sup>th</sup> March
1798 aged 22 years.

---

Here lieth the body of W<sup>m</sup> Long who died 5<sup>th</sup> June
1793 Æ 55 years, also 2 children, John & Mary.   Also
his wife, Jane Long, who died 4<sup>th</sup> Jan<sup>y</sup> 1838 aged 88
yr<sup>s</sup> & their son, William Long, who died 1<sup>st</sup> March 1861
aged 70 yr<sup>s</sup>.   Also his wife Anne died 3<sup>rd</sup> Feb<sup>y</sup> 1869
aged 72 years, also their daughter, Jane, died 6<sup>th</sup> Dec<sup>r</sup>
1875 aged 39 years and Eliza died 21<sup>st</sup> March 1876
aged 48 years.

---

Here lieth the body of Alex<sup>r</sup> Brennan who departed this
life 10<sup>th</sup> March 1787 aged 52 years.   Also his wife,
Abigail Wilson, who deceased 10<sup>th</sup> January 1807 aged
69 years Likewise their son, Joseph Brennan, who died
24<sup>th</sup> May 1824 aged 64 years.   Also two of his brothers,
Ja<sup>s</sup>. & W<sup>m</sup>, and of their sister, Sarah Brennan who died
7<sup>th</sup> June 1847 aged 82 years.   Likewise Thomas Brannan
who died 18<sup>th</sup> August 1851 aged 78 years.

---

' This stone is inscribed on both sides.   Older inscription ' :—

Here lyeth the body of Henry Brynan who departed
this life 3<sup>rd</sup> July 1753 aged 53 years.   Also his wife,
Sarah Brynan, who departed this life April 12<sup>th</sup> 1786
aged 77 years.   Also Jenny Neiper, wife to William
Brennan, who departed this life 1<sup>st</sup> November 1818,
aged 68 years.   Likewise the aforesaid W<sup>m</sup> Brennan
who died 28<sup>th</sup> January 1837 aged 83 years.   Also
Thomas Hill Brennan Kain who died 23<sup>rd</sup> February
1837 aged 7 months & of Sarah Brennan Kain, sister
of the above Thomas, who died 28<sup>th</sup> July 1842 aged 19
months.

' Newer inscription ' :—

Turned by William B. Cain in memory of his children
William Brennan Cain, ju<sup>r</sup> who died 4<sup>th</sup> Dec<sup>r</sup> 1858 aged
24 years.   Thomas Hill Brennan Cain died 23<sup>rd</sup> Feb<sup>ry</sup>
1857 aged 7 months & Sarah Brennan Cain died 28<sup>th</sup>
July 1842 aged 19 months.   Also their mother, Mary

Hill B Cain died 8<sup>th</sup> October 1864 aged 66 years also the above William B. Cain, their father, who died 8<sup>th</sup> August 1867 aged 72 years.

———

Erected by William Hamilton in memory of his wife, Abigaill Brennan, who departed this life 8<sup>th</sup> Janu<sup>y</sup> 1838 aged 34 years. Also the above named William Hamilton who departed this life in Glasgow on the 15<sup>th</sup> March 1878 aged 73 years.

———

Here lieth the body of Henry Branin who departed this life the 9<sup>th</sup> of May 1804 aged 57 years.

———

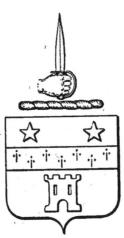

Here lyeth the body of Robert Kinkaid who dyed the 22 of Januar<sup>y</sup> 1697 aged 66 & also Agnas Donaldson, wife, who dyed the 27 of May 1718 aged 70 years and their son, Andrew Kinkaid who dyed the 18 of May 1725 aged 47 years. Also Cap<sup>tn</sup> John Kinkaid died January y<sup>e</sup> — 1730 aged 68 years.

' On top edge of stone ' :—

Who whilst (alive) will defend my life & honour to the end.

' A coat-of-arms is cut on the back of this stone.'

———

Here lyeth the body of George Kain who departed this life 25<sup>th</sup> Mar 1785 aged 62 years also his grandaug<sup>hr</sup>, Jenny Neiper Kain, who died the 19<sup>th</sup> Aug<sup>t</sup> 1804. Also Sarah Brennan, wife to John Kain, who died 12<sup>th</sup> April 1837 aged 73 years. Also the above John Kain who died 4<sup>th</sup> March 1844 Æ 79 years.

Here lyeth the body of Marth[a] Kein who died May 11
1752 aged 5 years. Also James Kein's wife, Janet
M^cIlwain, who died May 22^nd 1774 aged 56 years. Also
the above named James Kein who departed this life
30^th Nov^r 1793 aged 80 years.

---

Here lieth y^e body of John M^cDowall who departed this
life May y^e 22^d 1748 aged 72 years. Also his son Edw^d
M^cDowall who departed this life July y^e 13^th 1744 aged
34 years.

' On the back of this stone.'
Here lieth the body of George Allen who died in y^e year
1770 ÆT 9 mo^s. Robert Allen who died in July
1807 aged 27 years. John Allen who died Jan^y 12^th
1816 ÆT 36 years. George Allen died same year & mo
ÆT 40 years. Also their father John Allen died Nov.
7^th 1819 aged 90 years.

---

## Ballyprior Graveyard, Islandmagee.

[From Mr. W. F. Reynolds.]

' This graveyard lies at the north end of the peninsula, on
rising ground, commanding a fine view of the Antrim coast, from
Larne northwards. It is unsheltered by trees or shrubs, and
apparently contains no remains of an architectural nature. It is
thickly filled with graves; many of the stones, from their exposed
position, are so weather-worn that their inscriptions have long since

disappeared. A marked contrast exists here, as elsewhere, in the present condition of lettering, cut at about the same date, on slate and on the ordinary stone ; the former, after a little rubbing, shows clean, sharp edges, even the lighter incisions being distinct and legible, whereas the latter is blurred and difficult to follow ' :—

> Here lyeth the body of Alexander M$^c$Calmont who departed this life the 16$^{th}$ of September 1758 aged 38 years.

---

> [A winged hour-glass.]
>
> Here lyeth y$^e$ body of Margaret M$^c$N [in]ch who departed Oct y$^e$ 1$^{st}$ 1752 aged 67 years, late wife to Alexander M$^c$Kinstry.

---

> Here lyeth the body of Isabel Davison who departed this life 22$^{nd}$ Sep 1790 aged 79 years. She was wife to Hugh Jeffrey first and wife to Samuel Hill last.

---

> Here lyeth y$^e$ body of Mary Hill who died March y$^e$ 17$^{th}$ 1748 aged 49 years, late wife to Thomas Gillis who also died Feb$^r$ y$^e$ 21$^s$ 1766 aged 73 yr$^s$.

---

' This stone is inscribed on both sides ':—

> Here lyeth the body of Nathan Man who died Oct$^{br}$ the 10 1714 aged 66 years & Elizabeth Firrie his wife died Nov$^r$ y$^e$ 15 1724 aged 75 years with 8 sons & 7 daughters.

' On back of headstone : A shield, bearing three human legs conjoined in the fesse point at the upper part of the thighs and flexed in triangle. Underneath this the following inscription ' :—

> Here lyeth the body of Robert Man, son to the afore-menshened Nathan Man, y$^e$ said Robert departed this life May y$^e$ 11$^{th}$ 1737 aged 51 years.

---

> Here lieth the body of Jane Allen who dep$^t$ this life June the 14$^{th}$ 1779 aged 45 years. Also her husband James M$^c$Gown, who dep$^t$ this life April the 1$^{st}$ 1817 aged 88 years.

Here lyeth yᵉ bodies of William Davies who died Febʸ
20ᵗʰ 1736, aged 72 years also his brother John Davies.

———

Here lyeth the body of James Mᶜelwnes who died June
yᵉ 7ᵗʰ 1728 aged 35 years: also Catrien Sayer died
December 25 1729 : also John MᶜElwne died Febʳ yᵉ 5
1740 aged 77 years.

———

Set up by Joseph Gifford in memory of Elizabeth Gifford,
his wife, who died Janʸ 12ᵗʰ 1800 aged 40 years.   And
Martha, his mother, who died March 16ᵗʰ 1793 aged 63
years.   Here also are deposited the remains of the above
named Joseph Gifford who departed this life 27ᵗʰ August
1835 aged 66 years.

———

' In another part of the graveyard ' :—

Set up by Joseph Gifford in memory of Jane Gilliland
who died March 8ᵗʰ 1781 aged 5 years & Hugh Gilliland
who died 27ᵗʰ January 1795 aged 32 years.

———

Here lyeth the body of David Beggs who died March 30ᵗʰ
1798 in the 23ʳᵈ year of his age.

———

Here lyeth the body of William Wilson who died August
yᵉ 22ⁿᵈ 1703 & Jenet Wilson, his wife died July 20ᵗʰ
1704.

———

Here lyeth the body of Elizabeth Neeper who departed
this life August the 10ᵗʰ 1739 aged 23 years.   Also
William Neeper who depᵗ this life January 20ᵗʰ 1762
aged 9 years.

———

Here lyeth yᵉ bodies of James Bool who died Ocᵗ yᵉ 30ᵗʰ
1735 aged 95 years & his son, John, died June yᵉ 21ˢᵗ
1749 aged 80 years.   Also William Bool, son to John
Bool, died April yᵉ 29ᵗʰ 1757 aged 49 years.

Here lyeth yᵉ body of James Wilson who died Janʸ 15ᵗʰ 1732 aged 82 years. He had one son, viz, Joseph, who died abrod (*sic*).

---

' About the centre of the graveyard there is a large grave-space protected by iron railings. There are three stones—an upright one at the head, and two flat ones in the centre. The latter lie side by side, each being carried by six carved supports so that the lettered faces of the slab stand about 2½ feet above the surface of the ground. The supports belonging to the older slab have ornamented capitals. On the headstone the following inscription is clearly cut ' :—

Erected by Eliza Wilson in memory of her husband, Alexander Wilson, who died 31ˢᵗ January 1846 aged 49 years. And their son, Joseph, who died in infancy. Also in memory of her father, the Revᵈ John Murphy, 53 years minister of the Presbyterian Church, Island-magee, who died 12ᵗʰ June 1842 aged 87 years. Jane Brown, his wife died 29ᵗʰ April 1833 aged 78 years. Robert B. Murphy died 10ᵗʰ April 1813 aged 19 years. Margaret Murphy died 15ᵗʰ August 1841 aged 52 years. Archᵈ Dounan died 30ᵗʰ August 1850 aged 59 years.

---

' The older of the flat slabs measures 6 feet 2 inches long, 2 feet 8½ inches broad, and is 4½ inches thick. An ovolo, 1 inch broad, runs around the upper edge. On the surface two parallel lines are cut

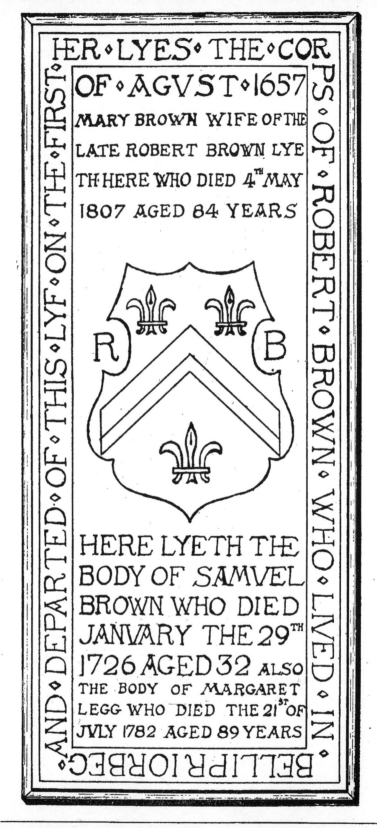

HER · LYES · THE · CORPS · OF · ROBERT · BROWN · WHO · LIVED · IN · BELLIPRIORBEC · AND · DEPARTED · OF · THIS · LYF · ON · THE · FIRST ·

OF · AGVST · 1657
MARY BROWN WIFE OF THE
LATE ROBERT BROWN LYE
TH HERE WHO DIED 4TH MAY
1807 AGED 84 YEARS

R    B

HERE LYETH THE
BODY OF SAMVEL
BROWN WHO DIED
JANVARY THE 29TH
1726 AGED 32 ALSO
THE BODY OF MARGARET
LEGG WHO DIED THE 21ST OF
JVLY 1782 AGED 89 YEARS

THE BROWN SLAB (1657) IN THE CHURCHYARD
OF BALLYPRIOR. CO. ANTRIM.

$3\frac{1}{4}$ inches apart, the outer one being $\frac{3}{4}$ inch distant from edge of ovolo. These lines are continued around the stone, and so form a border within which the following inscription appears ' ·—

HER · LYS · THE · GORPS · OF · ROBERT · BROWN ·
WHO · LIVED · IN · BELLIPRIORBEG · AND · DE-
PARTED · OF · THIS · LYF · ON · THE · FIRST ·
[The remainder of this part of the inscription is cut across the stone] OF · AVGST · 1657·

Mary Brown, wife of the late Robert Brown, lyeth here who died 4th May 1807 aged 84 years,

' In the middle of the slab a shield of arms, of unusual outline, is carved. On either side of the centre of this shield are the initials R. B. The bearings are : A chevron, between three fleurs-de-lys. Underneath ' :—

Here lyeth the body of Samuel Brown who died January the 29 1726 aged 32, Also the body of Margaret Legg, who died the 21st of July 1782 aged 89 years.

' The carvings and lettering on this stone are beautifully executed, and in an excellent state of preservation.
' The neighbouring slab bears, at its head, the same arms, with the addition of helmet, mantling, and crest : a goat statant ppr. The inscription on it is ' :—

HERE LYETH THE BODY OF JAMES BROWN, OF
BALLYPRIORBEGG, WHO DECEASED SEPTEMBER THE
10TH 1695 ÆTATIS 73 ALSO JEAN METCHIL, HIS
WIFE WHO DIED THE 16TH NOVEBR 1687 & THAY
HAD 5 SONS & 6 DAUGHTERS· ALSO WILLIAM
BROWN OF BALLIPRIORBEGG WHO DIED MARGH
THE 30TH 1738 AGED 80 YEARS AND JANET
MARTEN, HIS WIFE, DIED JULY THE 30TH 1740
AGED 80 YEARS· ALSO JANET BROWN WHO
DIED AUGUST THE 23RD 1753 AGED 8 MONTHS
DAUGHTER TO ROBERT BROWN OF BALLYPRIOR-
BEGG WHO ALSO DIED MAY THE 21ST 1758 AGED
33 YEARS. MARY MURPHY LIETH HERE WHO DIED
29TH JULY 1804 AGED 14 YEARS. MATTHW MURPHY
LIETH HERE WHO DIED 20TH MAY 1809 AGED 16
YEARS.

## Bonamargy Churchyard.

[Sent by Mr. J. W. Kernohan.]

Alexander M<sup>c</sup> | Curdys of Drimaha | mmon Burying pl | ace the 8<sup>th</sup> Sept<sup>br</sup> | 1792.

I H S

Erected | to the memory of | John M<sup>c</sup>Kinley late of the | Quay who departed this life the | 17<sup>th</sup> of June 1853 aged 63 years. | May he rest in peace Amen | and | his wife Mary died 1866 | aged 73 years.

Here lieth | the body of | Arch<sup>d.</sup> Whiteford | of Garta-lorkan | who departed this. | life the 8<sup>th</sup> Nov<sup>r</sup> | 1809 aged 49 years.

Here lyeth the body of Archba | ld M<sup>c</sup>Kwon who de | parted this life | Desmber the 19<sup>th</sup> | 1756 aged 60 Th | is is the buring | place of Dugell | M<sup>c</sup>Kwon and fa | mily.

Erected | by | Charles Jolly | of Drumahamon | In memory of his son | John Jolly | who departed this life | the 2<sup>nd</sup> of Sept<sup>r</sup> 1838 | aged 18 years.

The burying place of | Robert Blake of Ballycastle and family.

Sacred | to the memory of | Robert Black late of | Bally-castle who departed this | life 11<sup>th</sup> of January 1845 | aged 74 years | Also his wife Catherine who | departed this life 11<sup>th</sup> of Febr<sup>y</sup> 1837 | aged 63 years.

The burying | place of | Daniel M<sup>c</sup>Clarty who departed this | life the 20<sup>th</sup> day of | May 1808 aged 40 years.

To mark the ground | of Dennis M<sup>c</sup>Auley of | Cullaveely the remains of his wife Catherine | are here deposited on | the 5<sup>th</sup> January 1811 aged 69 | Erected by his son John.

Here | lyeth the bod | y of CATRIEN | WHYTE who |
departed this | life March the | 25 1758 aged | 60
years.

---

IHS

In memory | of | James Keenan who died | 8<sup>th</sup> March
1860 aged 82 years | also his wife | Harriett Keenan
who died 11<sup>th</sup> June 1861 aged 49 years | also their son
John died 26<sup>th</sup> | Feb<sup>y</sup> 1839 aged 10 years | Their
daughter Harriett | died 5<sup>th</sup> May 1859 aged 33 years.

---

IHS

Erected | to the memory of | Alexander M<sup>c</sup>Alister |
late of Ballynagard | who departed this | life on the
14<sup>th</sup> day of September Anno Domini 1858 aged 77
years.

---

Here | lyeth the body of | Hugh Hill who died April y<sup>e</sup>
. . . 1732 | aged [15 ?] years also John Hill . . .

---

1756.

NEAL<sup>x</sup> M<sup>c</sup>NEAL<sup>x</sup> | Apointed burying | place and his
family.

---

Here lieth | the body of Mur | phy M<sup>c</sup>Duffee wh | o
died the 24<sup>th</sup> | day of March 1760 | aged 70 years |
Done by order of his son Neal M<sup>c</sup>Duffee.

---

Arch<sup>d</sup> M<sup>c</sup>Lain's Burying Place.

---

Erected to the memory of | Randall M<sup>c</sup>Lister of Torr
who died 28<sup>th</sup> Oct<sup>r</sup> 1808 aged 58 years.

---

Roger M<sup>c</sup>Farland | burying place of | Ballycastle Here
lyeth the body | of John M<sup>c</sup>Farland | who departed
this | life May 9<sup>th</sup> 1773 | eaged 9 years.

[Fine red sandstone monument.]

This stone restored | in memory of | Coll M Donnell who | died 20<sup>th</sup> Jan<sup>ry</sup> 1773 aged | 61 years | Also his grandson Alex<sup>r</sup> | M<sup>c</sup>Donnell who died 8<sup>th</sup> | March 1868 aged 59 years | and his son Randall M<sup>c</sup> | Donnell who died 14<sup>th</sup> June 1871 | aged 33 years.

---

' The headstone adjoining the previous one has ' :—

Sacred to the memory of Alex<sup>r</sup> M<sup>c</sup> | Donnell late of Ballycastle | who departed this life 29<sup>th</sup> | Dec<sup>r</sup> 1813 aged 44 also his | wife Helen who departed this | life 11<sup>th</sup> Nov<sup>r</sup> 1838 aged 65 years | This stone erected through ¦ filial and piety [*sic*] of there son Alex<sup>r</sup>.

---

### 1764.

Alexander M<sup>c</sup>Donnell | wrought this monument for his family. Here ly | eth his daughter Frances M<sup>c</sup>Donnell who died | May the 13<sup>th</sup> 1763 Aged 3 | quarters.
[With arms at top.]

---

### 1788.

Con O'Sheil's | appointed bury | ing place and his family.

---

Here lieth the body | of James Hyndman | who departed this | life the 11<sup>th</sup> day of | October 1779 aged 57 | years.

---

### 1779.

James M<sup>c</sup> | Atyre's Burying | place of Broom | beg

---

Here lieth the body | of Daniel Roe M<sup>c</sup>Cor | mick of Murloch who | died Feb 4<sup>th</sup> 1800 aged 74.

---

Here | lieth the bo | dy of William M<sup>c</sup> | Elroy who died | the 16<sup>th</sup> of March | 1771 aged 76 years | Erected by John O'Haran.

---

✝

### I H S

Erected | in memory of John M<sup>c</sup>Killop | of Knocka-hara and family | A.D 1841 | " May they rest in peace, Amen."

Burying place of . . . Williamson's family.  Memento
Mori | I heard a voice from Heaven | saying unto me
write hence | forth, Blessed are the dead | which die in
the Lord even | so saith the Spirit for they | rest from
their labours | Rev. 14 c. 13 v. | Here lieth the body of |
Sarah Williamson who | departed this life the | 12ᵗʰ day of
June Aɴ. D. 1787 | aged 16 years, also of her son John
who died two days before her.

———

Here lie the body of Ann | wife of John Dunlop of |
Carverory who died 7ᵗʰ April | 1831 aged 39 years.

———

Dinnes Wilkeson's burrying place Here | lieth yᵉ body
of Daniel Wilkeson | who died July yᵉ | 13ᵗʰ 1767 aged 2
years.

———

The burying place | of Samˡ· Brown and fami | ly Here
lyeth the body of Neale Brown Mary Brown & Jas.
Brown.

———

Erected | by Alexander MᶜCay | of Carneymoon to the
memory | of his father John MᶜCay who | departed this
life on the 14ᵗʰ | day of May 1848 aged 64 years | Also
his nephew John Braizer ! who departed this life on the |
8ᵗʰ day of Febʳ 1851 aged 8 years.

✝
I H S

Erected in memory of | John MᶜAllester of Broughmore
who | departed this life 17ᵗʰ | July 1830 aged 80 years |
Also his wife Sarah who | died 17ᵗʰ April 1848 | aged 80
years | Also his son Archᵈ· MᶜAllester | died 1868 aged
80 years | and his wife Rose MᶜAllester | died 1874 aged
65 years.

———

Sacred | to the memory of John | Sharp late of Craig-
fad | who departed this life | the 14ᵗʰ of Mrh 1820 aged |
55 years also his wife | Katharine Sharp who | died in
1817 aged 50 years.

———

This stone was erected by | Daniel MacKey of Gart-
conney | in memory of his daughter Mary | MacKey who
departed this life | the 8ᵗʰ day of November 1809 | aged
26 years also Patrick | Mackey brother to the | above

named Daniel MacKey | who departed this life the 19<sup>th</sup> day of December 1815 aged 76 years. This burying ground | is now the property of | Hamilton Blackham | grandson of the above named D. M<sup>c</sup>K.

---

' Inside Abbey Church ' :—

Here | lieth the body | of Eneas Laver | ty who departed this life October | the 4<sup>th</sup> 1771 aged 55 | years also his daughter Mary who died March the 3<sup>rd</sup> | 1799 aged 35 years The above lived in Islandmagallan.

---

The burial place of Neale M<sup>c</sup>Neile of Colliershall and Alexander M<sup>c</sup>Neile of Ballycastle.

---

Here lyeth the | bodies of Captain Stewart | of Dun | dermot and family | and Francis Stew | art Bishop of Down | & Connor 1749.

---

' North of Church ' :—

Sacred to | the memory of | John M<sup>c</sup>Neille | late | of pounds who died 22<sup>d</sup> | Jan. 1836 aged 87 years | also his son Alex<sup>r</sup> M<sup>c</sup>Neille late of Greenock who died 31<sup>st</sup> May 1839 aged 31 years.

---

' East of church ' :—

Here lyeth the body | of John Daragh who died | August y<sup>e</sup> 15 1745 aged 1 | year also Ester Daragh died May y<sup>e</sup> 22, 1741 | aged ? years children to Archie Daragh also the s<sup>d</sup> Archibald | died April the 11<sup>th</sup> 1762 aged 45 years.

---

## Carrickfergus Church.

### [Mrs. T. Long.]*

' Over the mayor's seat ' :—

THIS WORKE BEGAN A,D, 1614, MR. COOPER THEN MAYOR, AND WROUGHT BY THOMAS PAPS FREE MASON, MR. OPEN-SHAWE BEING PARSON, VIVAT REX JACOBUS.

---

* Copied from M'Skimin's "History of Carrickfergus."

'Stone on south wall':—

> HERE LIETH THE BODY OF THOMAS COUPER ALDERMAN AND
> TWIS MAIRE OF CARICKFERGUS DESESED THE 20ᵀᴴ OF
> AUGUST 1625.

[This stone has the arms of Couper and Ratcliffe impaled.]

---

'On north wall':—

> HERE LIETH THE BODY OF | ROBERT OPENSHAWE MINISTER, |
> DEAN OF THE CATHEDRAL CHURCH | OF ST. SAVIOUR'S OF
> CONNER | IN THE COUNTY OF ANTRIM, TO | THE TOWN OF
> CRAGFERGUS PASTOR, AND CHAPLAYNE TO THE RIGHT HONᴮᴸᴱ
> LORD CHICHESTER BARON OF | BELFAST & LORD HIGH
> TREASURER OF IRELAND    DIED . . . 1627.

---

'On a coffin':—

> THE MOST HONOURABLE THE LADY | MARCHIONESS OF
> ANTRIM RELICT | OF THE | MOST HONOURABLE RANDALL |
> MC | DONNELL MARQUIS & EARL OF ANTRIM VISCOUNT
> DUNLUCE AND SOLE | DAUGHTER AND HEIR OF SIR HENRY
> O' | NEILL OF EDENDUFF-CARRICK IN THE | COUNTY OF
> ANTRIM, WHO DEPARTED | THIS LIFE AT EDENDUFF-CARRICK
> AFORESAID | ON THE 27ᵀᴴ DAY OF APRIL ANNO | DOMINI
> 1695, IN THE 64 YEAR OF HER AGE.

---

> HERE LYETH THE BODY | OF EDMOND DAVY ALDERMAN |
> TWICE MAYOR OF CARRICKFERGUS | WHO DEPARTED THIS |
> LIFE THE 6ᵀᴴ DAY OF JULY | ANNO DOM 1696 IN | THE 73
> YEAR OF | HIS AGE.
> HERE ALSO LYETH MARY | HIS WIFE KATHERINE, ANN, |
> MARTHA, EDMOND, EZEKIEL, | AND NATHANIEL, SONS AND |
> DAUGHTERS OF Yᴱ SAID, | EDMOND AND MARY, | BEING
> DESCENDED OF A BRANCH | OF THE ANCIENT FAMILY OF
> GUSTANNA | NORTH WALES.

---

> HERE LYETH | THE BODY OF HENRY | CLEMENTS OF STRADE |
> ESQ. AGED 52 YEARS | WHO DEPARTED THIS LIFE | THE 2ᴺᴰ
> DAY OF NOVEMBER | 1696 BEING THEN | MAYOR OF CARRICK-
> FERGUS.

[This slab cannot now be found.]

---

A large flag on the floor bore an inscription to Mary
Williamson & others of her family, date 1674.
[Cannot now be found.]

This font, a silver | fiagon, the tables | of the command-
ments | Lord's Prayer and creed, were given | to this
Church by Samuel Davys | Alderman | Anno Dom,
1714.

---

Here lyeth y$^e$ | Body of Eliz | abeth Hill who | de-
parted this | life y$^e$ 9 of Dec$^r$ | 1726, aged 50 | years. |
Here also lyeth y$^e$ body of Ann | her daughter | who
departed | Y$^e$ 10.$^{th}$ of Nov$^r$, 1720 | Aged 22 years.

---

' On a coffin ' :—

The Right Honourable and Illustrious | Katherine
Countess of Donegall Dowager of | the Most Noble and
Puissant Arthur | Chichester late Earl of Donegall |
Viscount Carrickfergus, Lord Chichester, Baron of
Belfast. Died June 15$^{th}$ 1743 | aged 73 years.

---

Here lieth the body of the | Rev$^d$, Hill Benson, Dean of
Connor. | He was born the 3$^{rd}$ of October, 1704, and |
departed this life the 21$^{st}$ of April | 1775. | They that
be wise shall shine as the brightness of the firmament
and they that turn many to righteousness as the stars
for ever and ever.

---

Near this place lies interred | the body of | Captain
Charles Stewart | 5$^{th}$ Lord Molesworths Dragoons | son
of Alexander Stewart, of Wester, | Cluny | Perthshire, |
and Isabella Stewart, of Ballnakillie, | his wife. | He
died 4$^{th}$ June, 1774, distinguished | alike in his military
& private career, | by his fidelity to the path of duty
and by his | display of every amiable and Christian
Virtue. | Also to the memory of | Rose his wife, | who
died 11$^{th}$ February, 1779, aged 92 years. | She was
daughter of Roger Hall. Esq, of Narrow-Water, Co,
Down, and granddaughter of | Sir Toby Poyntz, K$^{nt}$, of
Acton and | Brenagh, Co. Armagh.

---

Sacred | to the memory of | The Rev$^d$ Richard Dobbs,
A,M. | Dean of Connor; Whose life was devoted to a
faithful | & zealous discharge of pastoral duties, | Thro
a period of near Forty years. | Possessed of a temper
calm & deliberate | His calmness was the result of
firmness | of mind; and his deliberation wisdom. His
piety was unaffected & sincere | the Affections of his

heart strong and | Permanent | He was called | to receive the everlasting reward | of his pious & charitable labours | on the IV<sup>th</sup> day of Febry. MDCCCII | In the LXI, year of his age | Multis ille bonis flebilis occidit.

————

This monument is inscribed | by a few of the friends of | Samuel Davys Steuart | of Carrickfergus M.D. | who | from a long and intimate knowledge | of his worth, offer it as a Faithful | tribute to his sacred memory. | It is consecrated by the tears of the | poor and the prisoner, to heal whose | bodily diseases, and to improve | whose moral condition, his eminent | professional talents, his enlightened, | understanding, and the feelings of | his benevolent heart, were applied. | Died November 4<sup>th</sup>, 1817 | aged 36 years.

————

Sacred to the memory | of | Lieutenant James Everard ; | William Todd, Robert Henderson, and John Boyd, | seamen of this place, late belonging to | His Majestys sloop "Nimrod," | who were drowned in Belfast Lough, | by the upsetting of a boat, August 15<sup>th</sup> 1825, | as a tribute of respect for | an amiable young man, and highly meritorious officer, | and for the worthy good seamen, | the Captain, officers and ships company of the Nimrod | have erected this tablet.

————

Sacred | to the memory of | Robert Hanly | who lived esteemed and died regretted | May 11<sup>th</sup> 1831. | This monument was erected by | Lord George A Hill | Representative for Carrickfergus, as a memorial of | his respect and regard.

————

In loving memory of | Surgeon Major | David Redmond Taggart, M.D. | Royal Antrim Artillery | and Coroner County Antrim and Carrickfergus, | died 10<sup>th</sup> April, 1886, aged 47 years. | Until the day break, and the shadows flee away."

————

Sacred | to the memory of | Blayney Townley Walshe, Esqr, | Late Lieut. Col. Royal Artillery, | who departed this life Jan, 29<sup>th</sup>, 1839, aged 62. | Also of Anna his wife, who died in Dublin, Jan. 18<sup>th</sup>, 1840, aged 49.

In memory of the Rev Bennett W. Jones. curate of |
Carrickfergus, through Divine grace a shining model of
a Christian pastor, and a meek and lowly servant of the
Lord Jesus Christ. This monument is raised by his
brethren in | the ministry and a sorrowing flock, to
record for a perpetual | example the faith and integrity
of a man of GOD, whose | animated zeal was not less
powerful to win souls then his | gentleness and loving
kindness to retain them. In the | inscrutable Provi-
dence of the Most High His faithful servant | was
called from his blessed labours whilst his usefulness
was | full of promise. Attacked by malignant fever in
Dublin, he died 27$^{th}$ May, 1841, in the second year of
his ministry, and 25$^{th}$ year of his age. The will of GOD
be done.

Sacred to the memory of | Henry Eccleston | who in
the 38$^{th}$ year of his age was drowned | off the Isle of
Barbuda, in the West Indies. His barque the "Lanca-
shire Witch" having been | wrecked in a hurricane on
the 18$^{th}$ August 1851. | This tablet is erected by his
widow, | Jane Eccleston | in remembrance of a beloved
husband | and affectionate father.

> "Far, far he lies from holy ground,
>     Deep in his coral bed ;
> The sea weeds wrap his corse around,
>     The waves roll o'er his head."

And the sea gave up the dead which were in it. |
Rev. 20 13.
Also his daughter Georgina, who died 10$^{th}$ May 1845, |
aged 3 years.

To the memory | of | Staff surgeon | John Millar, who
died at Glasgow, | May 3$^{rd}$ 1850, | aged 55 years. | In
affectionate remembrance | the officers who served with
him | in the 43rd Light Infantry | of which Regt. he
was surgeon | for 18 years | have erected this monu-
ment. | His remains rest in | Lighthill Cemetery, at
Glasgow.

In memory of | David Legg | Solicitor and Town Clerk |
of | Carrickfergus, | who died 20$^{th}$ March 1854, | aged
51 years. | A few attached friends | erected this tablet |
as a mark of their esteem.

Sacred to the memory of | John Edward Kidley M.D. |
who departed this life | 6<sup>th</sup> April | 1852 | and | Frances
Anne Kidley | who departed this life, | 17<sup>th</sup> June, 1852,|
son & daughter of John Kidley, | Of Fownhope,
Herefordshire, England. | Also, Jane Maxwell, Relict
of Surgeon Maxwell, | who departed this life | 27<sup>th</sup>
December, 1844. | Also of Sarah Eliza Kidley, | relict
of John Kidley Esq. | of Fownhope, Herefordshire, |
who departed this life | 1<sup>st</sup> January, 1855.

---

Erected by James Stephens | In memory of his father, |
Stratford Stephens, | who died 24<sup>th</sup> January, 1848, aged
48 years. | And in affectionate remembrance of his dear
Mother, | Margaret Stephens, | Who died 18<sup>th</sup> April,
1873, aged 67 years. | Deeply regretted by her children
for whom | her love and devotion were unbounded.

---

In loving memory | of | Robert Rowan, | Late Captain
52<sup>nd</sup> Oxfordshire Light Infantry, | Born 17<sup>th</sup> March,
1780, at Bellisle, | County Antrim, | Died 6<sup>th</sup> January
1863, at Carrickfergus. | And of | Henrietta Maria, his
wife, | born 20<sup>th</sup> of November, 1814, at Waterford, |
died 9<sup>th</sup> March, 1879, at Carrickfergus. | In the world
ye shall have tribulation ; | but be of good cheer, I have
overcome the world." John 16. 33.

---

### RECTORS.

1503 John Cautok.
1573 . . . Darsye.
1590 Edward Edgeworth.
1596 John Tedder (or Charden, made Bishop of Down
          and Connor, 1593; there appears to be a
          mistake in these dates)
1599 Hugh Griffith.
1609 Miles Whaly.
1615 Robert Openshaw.
1628 Richard Shugborrough, alias Shugburgh.
1658 Robert Price, 1660, Leighlin and Ferns ; died 1666.
1660 Francis Marsh, later Dean of Armagh, Bishop of
          Limerick, then of Kilmore and Ardagh, and
          finally of Dublin ; died 1693.
1661 George Rust, Bishop of Dromore, 1667.

Rectors—continued.

1667 Patrick Sheridan, afterwards Bishop of Cloyne, died 1682.
1679 Thomas Ward.
1694 George Story.
1706 Martin Baxter.
1710 Owen Lloyd, died 1743.
1743 John Walsh, died 1753.
1753 Hill Benson, died 1775.
1775 Richard Dobbs, died Feb. 1802.
1802 Thomas Graves.
1811 Theophilus Blakely.
1825 Henry Lesley.
1839 John Chaine.
1855 George Bull, D.D.
1886 George Chamberlain.
1908 Rev. F. J. M'Neice.

' These are from M'Skimin's "History of Carrickfergus." '—
A. Long.

## Duneane Church.

' Brass tablet, inside church, on north wall.
' Coat-of-arms and crest (Hamilton-Jones) on left corner ;
monogram on right corner :—" Shako on drum, sword, bayonet,
rifles, and colours, enclosed in a laurel wreath." '

> Sacred to the Memory of Colonel John Charles Hill
> Morres Jones late of the 54th regiment born at
> Moneyglass in the County Antrim March 30th 1824,
> died very suddenly on Sunday September 3rd 1876 at
> Wavertree while in command of the 13th & 14th
> Brigade Depots and of the troops in Liverpool. This
> tablet is erected by his wife in loving and sorrowful
> remembrance and in testimony of the deep and universal
> regret felt at his death by all who knew him. Thou
> art my hiding place and shield : I hope in thy word.
> Psalm cxix. v. 114. Luke x. 30-37.

' The above Colonel Morris-Jones was only and younger brother
to the late Thomas Morris-Hamilton-Jones, of Moneyglass, County
Antrim.'

# COUNTY ARMAGH.

## Mullaghbrack Churchyard.

[From the Rev. J. B. Leslie, Rector of Kilsaran.]

' The inscription, which appears below, is copied from a flat slab in this churchyard; it is cut in raised Roman capitals round the edge, and continues across the stone thus ' :—

TIOIM · THE · BODIE · OF · IAMIS · AYISIN · GALBRAIT · GVVD

MAN · OF · BATGAIR ·

MENTO MORI

AYISIN ANNO DOMINI · 1618 ÆTATIS SVE

[ Break ]    ] 3 · THE · IN · LYFE · THIS · DEPAIRTID · WHA

'Owing to a break in the slab, the inscription is incomplete. The first word (if perfect) is unintelligible; and the AYISIN, which occurs twice in the inscription, is puzzling. All the N's are reversed on the slab.

# COUNTY CARLOW.

## Tullow Churchyard.

[Contributed by Miss A. Peter, from an old notebook of 1837.]

HERE LIETH THE BODY OF M^RS MARY LYNEALL WHO DEPARTED THIS LIFE THE 19^TH DAY OF NOVEMBER 1682. AND OF THOMAS LYNEALL HER HVSBAND WHO DEPARTED THIS LIFE THE 9^TH DAY OF IVLY 1692, AND BENJAMIN LYNEALL, THE SON OF THOMAS & MARY LYNEALL WHO DEPARTED THIS LIFE 4^TH DAY OF MARCH 1707

HERE LIETH THE REMAINS OF
NICHOLAS REALLY WHO DEPARTED
10TH OF OCTOBER 1673.

---

THE FAMILY CEMETERY
OF PONSONBY SHAW, ESQR, FRIARSTOWN.
THIS MONUMENT IS ERECTED BY HIM
IN MEMORY OF HIS DAUGHTER MATILDA
WHG DIED 17TH DAY OF MARCH 1833
AGED 23 YEARS

---

UNDER THIS STONE ARE DEPOSITED
THE REMAINS OF
FRANCES
FOR FIFTY YEARS THE FAITHFUL & AFFECTIONATE
WIFE OF BERESFORD BURSTON OF FIRR
HOUSE, ESQR, SHE DEPARTED THIS
LIFE THE 21ST OF JANUARY 1824
IN THE 81 YEAR OF HER AGE.

---

## COUNTY CAVAN.

---

### Bailieborough Presbyterian Churchyard.

[From Mr. Thomas Hall.]

This Stone is Erected in Memory
of Mary Wife of Henry Adams of
Bailieborough who died on the
Second of June 1847 aged 46
Years
Underneath is also deposited the
Mortal Remains of Henry Adams of
Bailieborough Who died on the 23rd
July 1858 Aged 61 Years

---

In memory of
WILLIAM WHITE
of Pottle
who died May 1835
aged 85 years
He was for forty years a Ruling Elder
in the Congregation of Corglass

Also of
ELIZABETH WHITE
his wife
Who died November 1840
aged 87 years
Erected
in fulfilment of the wishes
of their Son
PATRICK WHITE

---

This Monument Was here place<sup>d</sup>
in memory of James Rusk of gralo<sup>gh</sup>
Who departed this life the 24<sup>th</sup> day
of 8b<sup>r</sup> A.D. 1791 Aged 72 Years
Also his Wife Mary Rusk Who
Departed this life the    day of
A.D.  -  Aged    years

' NOTE.—The wife's age, &c., was never inserted.'

---

Sacred to the Memory
of
Eliezer Gilmer of Lear Who Departed
this life on the 5<sup>th</sup> day of January 1849
Aged 81 Years
also to
George Gilmer Son to the above who
Departed this life on the 11<sup>th</sup> of May
1857 Aged 63 Years.

# COUNTY CLARE.

### Clondagad Church.
[From Mr. T. J. Westropp.]

' The parish is first mentioned as Clondagah and Eribanub in the Papal Taxation of 1302. The last name is probably "Scribanus," to be connected with the well named Toberscreabaun in the parish. The name Clondagad belongs to the form, so common in this country (like Glendalough, Clondanagh, &c.), marking the strange regard of the Irish for the number two. Legend says in this case that Clondagad, the plain of the two gads (or withes), derived its name from two druids, Screabaun and Fiddaun, having contested with each other in magic, making their "gads" float up the stream—no great miracle in the tidal part—and Screabaun won. A rock recess or bed of Screabaun is shown near the river. The ancient church has left no trace; and the present one, with its rounded "corners" and western belfry, is very modern, having been rebuilt in 1809. We collected the following epitaphs, but not a few others are defaced or partly covered; none of these latter seemed of any great age':—

1.　CONNOR CONSI | DYNE MARG B.　1631.

'It is on a flat tapering stone, now broken, with a neat, slightly rounded moulding at the edge; the date is at the narrower end, both facing the broader end; the wife's name does not appear to have been completed. It has been removed, and the fragments lie on modern graves close together.'

2. ' Canon Dwyer gives the following, which I failed to find ':—

Stand passenger, gaze & see | such as I am so shalt thou bee who died to live so live to die | Depart, muse on eternity.　M$^r$ Robt Smith departed this life 17$^{th}$ Feb 1676

3. ' " Crest : a peacock.　Arms (Ross) : three water budgets impaling (Harrison) a bend charged with three escallops, between two lions rampant.　All in a lozenge " ' :—

Within this burying place | lyes enterred the body of | George Ross Esq$^{re}$ who was | founder thereof he dyed | the 19$^{th}$ of May 1700 in the 79 (?) | yeare of his age This monument was erected | the same yeare by the order | of his kindsman Robert | Harrison.*

' The will of George Ross is extant (March 11th, 1699, proved at Dublin, Prerogative, June 15th, 1700).　He left Fortfergus and other lands to John Lewin, son of Barbara Lewin, sister of Robert Harrison, of Bishop Auckland, Durham, on condition of John taking the extra name of Ross.　Lewin is ancestor of the Ross Lewins of Fortfergus, and Ross Hill, County Clare.　The inscription is on a plain mural monument set, above the burial enclosure, in the south wall of the church.'

---

* The copy on p. 73 of Frost's " History of Clare " is inaccurate.

4. I.H.S.  HERE LIETH THE BODY OF | LUKE CORY OF LANA
WHO | DEPARTED THIS LIFE THE 10ᵀᴴ | AUGUST 1709 IT
BEING THE 67ᵀᴴ | YEAR OF HIS AGE.

' It lies at the south-west angle of the graveyard, and is cut in
capital letters.'

---

5. HERE LYETH THE BODY | OF WILLIAM WATERS WHO | DE-
PARTED THIS LIFE THE | 30ᵀᴴ OF 8BOR 1759 | AGED 63
YEARS.  GOD HAVE | MERCY ON HIM AND HIS POSTERITY
AMEN.

' To south-west of church.'

---

6.  + I. H. S. THIS TOMB WAS | ERECTED BY FLAN | MULUIHILL
FOR HIS | WIFE BRIDGETT MULUIHILL | ALIAS CREAGH
WHO DIED THE 3D DAY OF DECEMBER | 1763 ADGED FIFTY |
FOUR THE LORD HAVE | MERCY ON HER SOUL AMEN AND
ON [the rest very small, though plenty of room remains]
her posterity.

' West side of graveyard.'

---

7. Here lies the body of | Michˡ Scanlon who | died March
17ᵗʰ 1779 | Aged 7 years Erected by | his father Batt
Scan | lon of Clondrina for | him & his posterity |
Requiescat in pace | Amen | Batt Scanlon died | Jan 4ᵗʰ
1817 Aged | 76 yrs Erected by | his son | Thomˢ.

' East side of graveyard.'

---

8. This | Monument Was | erected by Mʳ Henry | White-
stone in memory | of his wife Mʳˢ Catherine Whitestone
Alias Lucas who died | The 9ᵗʰ of Dec 1782, aged 65
years.

' On the end of a vault attached to the west wall of the belfry
with neat rusticated arch, urns, and arched tablet.'

---

9. I. H. S. | Here lies the body of Penny Browne, Al Mᶜ |
Mahon, who Depᵈ this | Life Oct 19ᵗʰ 1788 Aged | 31
yʳˢ Erectᵈ by her son Nicholas Brown (sic) | For him
and Posterity.

' Near last.'

10. Here lies the body of | James Considine | who departed this life | Jan 24ᵗʰ 1790 | Aged 40 yʳ Erected | by his wife Bridget | Courcy for her and posterity May they | rest in peace, Amen

---

11. I.H.S. | Here lies the body of | Mich Doody died May 4ᵗʰ 1797 | aged 85 years. Erected by | his Brother Thady Doody | For him and family | May they rest in peace Amen.

---

' The following tombs later than 1800 were noted.'

12. Patrick Ronan Nov 1808

' Much worn.'

---

13. Timothy Quailly died March 7ᵗʰ 1809 aged 66, by his son Timothy.

---

14. Martin Sexton died Feb 2ⁿᵈ 1809 aged 17, by his brother Patrick.

---

15. Mary Corry, alias Chambers, died Ap 1811 aged 30. By her husband Michˡ.

---

16. John Scanlan, died 1819. [worn] Patrick D. Scanlon.

---

17. John Coffee, died June 27ᵗʰ 1823, aged 51. By his son Michˡ.

---

18. Mary Brown, alias Griffin, died Ap. 17. 1830 aged 21 by her brothers Mich. & Lott.

---

19. Mary Duhan (?) died June 27. 1833 aged 18 by her father Michˡ.

---

20. James & Daniel Kenedy. John Kennedy died March 30, 1834 aged 24.

' It has a curious group, frequently found in the period 1820–50, in Munster :—The crucifixion, I.N.R.I., sun and moon overhead, thirty pieces of silver, fifteen to each side, angel with trumpet, scales, coffin, and spear to right; hammer, pincers, nails, cock crowing out of pot, and St. Peter in profile, with bishop's mitre, and the two keys to left. A somewhat similar group is on John Daly's tomb, 1839.'

---

21. Bridget OShea alias Ronan died Feb 23. 1836 aged 39. By her husband James Shea (*sic*) of Tubber.

---

22. Mich¹ Daly to his brother Patrick who died Nov 8ᵗʰ 1839

---

23. John Daly, 1839, : Patt, 1845, aged 41 & Mary, 1846, aged 31.

---

25. I.H.S. Revᵈ Garrett OShaughnessy | for 30 years P.P. of Clondegad | died September the 20ᵗʰ | 1846 Aged 62 years.
'Near west end of church.'

---

26. Dan¹ Kelly d. May 5ᵗʰ 1858, aged 23. By his father Tim Kelly, of Clare Castle.
'It has a ship in full sail, carved at foot, and the words, "The Master of the Mariner."'

---

27. Anstance Dillon [No date].

---

28. [Cross and urns] James & Dan Crowe to their father James d. Ap 27ᵗʰ 1866 aged 65 and mother Susan died Ap 11ᵗʰ 1877 aged 72.

---

29. [I.H.S. and urns] John King of Ballyclohesy died 26 Aug 1866, aged 68, by his son Patrick.

---

30. Michael John Kirrane of Furroor to his father Patrick died March 1877 aged 72.

---

31. James Corry of Lissycasy to his father John Corry died March 7. 1892 aged 75

'There are a few still more recent crosses. It is interesting to note the fashion in monuments "in this neglected spot." The formulas of the inscriptions hardly vary from 1709 to 1866. It is also noteworthy that only in one instance is a clergyman of either denomination represented by a monument. The places of residence only appear in the modern tombs, with one exception, in 1709, and another probably in 1817.'

## Killone Abbey.

[From Mr. T. J. Westropp.]

'On the opposite page is shown the mural monument of the Lucas family.

'The inscription on it appeared on p. 393 of the third volume of the JOURNAL ; and the arms at p. 385, fig. vii, on Plate II.

'The tomb was erected in 1763.'

# COUNTY CORK.

## Ballyfeard.

[From James Coleman, M.R.S.A.I.]

'Ballyfeard graveyard occupies a rather unique position, being in the centre of the little village which lies five miles south of Carriga-line Railway Station. There is no trace of the church which must have stood here ; and there are no trees in the graveyard. Graves occupy its central portion, and only about twenty bear inscribed headstones, nearly all of them being of recent date. The following are the most interesting inscriptions that came under my notice here ' :—

> Erected | in memory of | Michael Leahy of Kilpatrick | who died Sep 10 | 1855. Aged 82 years | By his daughter Mrs. Mary Barrett of Massachusetts | May he rest in peace. Amen.

> Sacred | to the memory of Daniel Coveney | who departed this life | March 16, 1823 Aged 40 years | Erected by his beloved wife Mary | as an everlasting memorial of her affection | Peace to his immortal soul and may it rest | in blissful heaven | with angels always blest.

THE LUCAS MONUMENT AT KILLONE ABBEY,
CO. CLARE.

[From a photograph by Mr. T. J. Westropp.]

## Castlemartyr Church.

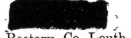

[From Rev. Henry B. Swanzy, Omeath Rectory, Co. Louth.]

The Pratt mural monument in Castlemartyr Church is surmounted by the crest: an elephant's head, an urn, and a snake,
with tail in mouth.   Below are the Pratt arms.

' Robert Pratt, to whose memory this monument was erected,
was son of James Pratt, of Carricknashinny, near Youghal, County
Cork, Bailiff of Youghal, 1718; by Mary, daughter of Simon
Creen, of Youghal, Bailiff, 1696.   He was admitted Freeman of
Youghal 2nd April, 1739, and married, 1740, Sarah, daughter of
Richard Williams, of Ightermurrough, County Cork.   Several of
his descendants attained distinction, including his son, General
John Pratt, who, when Major, erected the monument to his father's
memory; and his grandson, General Sir Thomas Kenagh, K.C.B.;
his nephew, Lieut.-Col. Sir Charles Pratt, K.C.B., was baptized at
Castlemartyr 19th January 1775.

' The inscription on the monument runs ':—

Sacred
To the Memory of ROBERT PRATT, Efq.
who
departed this Life 5th of November 1793.
in the 80th year of his Age.
He fill'd the Office of Chief Magistrate of Castlemartyr near half a
century.
Those who knew him can but attest his many virtues.
In his private character he was of an Integrity Incorruptible.
A constant Benefactor to the Poor, and in him the Fatherlefs and
widow ever found a Friend and Benefactor.
As a Magistrate he was to a Surrounding Neighbourhood the Bond
of Union, Peace, and Happiness.
He lived in his humble sphere, a bright example of Philanthropy
and Benevolence.
He rejoiced in the succefs of honest Industry in others, and was
ever ready to promote it.
The Goodnefs of his heart incited his Benevolence, whilst the
Excellence of his Understanding enabled him to defcriminate.
His Virtues gain'd him the Affection and Esteem of Men, and he
paid to Heaven the moft sincere homage of a good Life.
This Monument was erected from Filial Piety and Gratitude to the
beft of Fathers by his Sons, the Revd JAMES PRATT, and Major JOHN
PRATT of the Royal Irish Artillery.

' Arms: Gules, on a fess or, three mullets sable, between as
many elephants' heads erased of the second.'

## Connell Churchyard.

[From Mr. C. J. Hobson, New York.]

'Within two miles of Queenstown is the ancient burial-ground of Connell. Unlike many of our old burial-places, it is well kept, and of considerable extent, a new portion having been added in recent years.

'In this burial-ground there is an ancient ruin, not of any architectural importance. In this old ruin there are a number of tombs and tablets. On the left side as you enter is the tomb of the author of the poem " The Burial of Sir John Moore." On the front panel are the words " Rev. Chas. Wolfe," while the inscription on top reads as follows :—

Here lie
The Remains of
The Rev Charles Wolfe
Late Curate of Donoughmore
Who died at Cove 21$^{st}$ Feb. 1823
Aged 31
The record of his genius
Piety and virtue
Lives in the hearts
Of all who knew him.
Looking unto Jesus he lived
—Looking unto Jesus he died
He is not dead but sleepeth.

———

'On the right as you enter is a marble tablet with coat-of-arms to the Countess of Huntingdon, also tomb. The inscription on the tablet is here given ' :—

ELIZABETH ANNE
COUNTESS
OF
HUNTINGDON
BORN 29TH OF MAY 1817
DIED FEB 18TH 1857
AGED 39
REV. XIV. 13 2ND COR. V. 1.

'Lady Huntingdon was the daughter and heir of Richard Power, Esq., M.P., of Clashmore, Co. Waterford.

'The following somewhat lengthy inscription is copied from a tablet on the south wall':—

Sacred to the memory
of
JOHN TOBIN Esq of Lincolns Inn
Whose remains are deposited under
the adjacent turf
He died at sea
Near the entrance of this Harbour
In the month of December
1804
On his passage to a milder climate
In search of better health
Aged 35.
That with an excellent heart
And a most amiable Disposition
He possessed a vigorous imagination
And a cultivated understanding
His Dramatic writings
evince.

———

'In the churchyard there are quite a number of interesting inscriptions. I had only time to copy the following two. Of the inscriptions in the churchyard that of Stephen Towse situated against the wall at the door of the old church, is the most interesting. The stone is of limestone, and the inscription, except the figure 8 in the age, and figure 3 in the date, is quite legible. It will be noticed that only the age in the second part of the inscription is given, while the sculptor has made a liberal use of capitals and small letters, mixing them up in the inscription to suit his fancy. In every instance the letter D is given as a small letter, also the letter H, except when used as an initial letter. The letters H and E in the word "her" in the second last line are conjoined, the only instance of this kind made use of in the inscription. The final letter in the wife's Christian name is also omitted':—

Here Lyeth The Body
Of Stepen Towse Who
departed This life The
26 day of October 1698
ALso HIs wife ELIZ
Towse Who departEd
Her Life the 10 day of
February ANd IN The
84 year of HEr AGE
ANno DomINI 1713.

[Masonic emblems.]
Here Lieth The Body of William
Knowles : Sail Maker From
*Liverpool* Who was Drownd
At Cove *October* 20<sup>th</sup> 1813 in
The 32<sup>nd</sup> Year of his Age.

' The above inscription is copied from a headstone at the top of
which there is a Bible, the all-seeing eye, square and compass, and
the level, all carved in relief.'

---

## Dungourney.

[From Mr. J. Coleman.]

' The graveyard at this place can be reached in an hour's walk
over a good but uphill road from Mogeely Station on the Cork and
Youghal line. This graveyard, in which stands the Protestant
church, a pretty little building with a spire to it, is rather small,
fairly well kept, and with but few gravestones of recent date, due
possibly to a diminished population. It lies at some distance south
of the village. The most notable inscription is that on a table-
tomb, in somewhat large lettering ' :—

Sacred | to the Memory | of Digby Foulke Esq | of
Young Grove | obiit January 17 1809 | Aetat suae 53 |
In him the poor have lost their liberal benefactor | The
tenant has lost his most indulgent | landlord | and his
children their fond their doating Father | God only can
console his afflicted widow | By inspiring her with
resignation to His will | while a momentary relief is
granted to her | suffering | by erecting this earthly
memorial | of her affection and Record of his worth.

---

Erected | by Laurence Condon of Monaloo | in memory
of his mother | Elizabeth Condon alias O'Neil |
departed this life Nov 8<sup>th</sup> 1831 | Aged 54 years.

---

Erected by James Mahony | of Killin | doling in memory
of his son | Andrew Mahony | who departed this life
September 29, 1819 | aged 28 years.

---

This stone was erected | By the sons of Maurice Connery
to his me | mory & as a mark of their Burial-place | He
died 7ber the 20<sup>th</sup>, 1790 [Remainder underground.]

Erected | by John Keeffe | of Glowntawn in memory of
his father John | Keeffe who departed this life | July
18th, 1834 | aged 35 years.

---

This | stone was erected by Daniel | Murphy and his
wife, Cathorine | Conry in memory of their son, William
who died January the | 4th 1798 | aged 25 years.

---

Erected | by Edward Coleben in memory of his |
daughter Mary who | died December 10th 1808 | aged
19 years.

---

Erected | by Margaret Keleher alias Long | in memory
of her husband | Timothy Keleher of Mogeela | who
died August 19th 1855 | aged 67 years.

---

Erected | By John Smithwick of Whiterock | as a
small tribute of esteem | and parental affection to his |
daughter Mary Smithwick | who died January 28, 1834
aged 17 years.

---

Here lieth the body of | Michael Smedy | who died
June ye 23rd 1803 | aged 72 years.

---

Here | lieth the body of | Simon Kerney who | departed
this life the 10th day of March 1782 | aged 73 years.

---

Erected by | Christopher Garde of Sleveen | in memory
of his Grandfather | Simon Kearney of Ballyrussell |
who died April 23rd 1833 aged 77 years | also his Grand-
mother Mary Kearney | died October 12th 1844 aged 80
years | Also his uncles | Maurice died December 9,
1837 | Patrick died August 6th 1846 | Andrew died
May 30, 1856 | William died March 9, 1860 | John
died December 20, 1868 | James died May 23, 1873 |
Simon died June 2, 1876.   R.I.P.

---

This | Stone was erected by | William Wall in Me |
mory of his father | Edmond who died Febray the 20th
1763 [Remainder underground.]

---

Here lieth the body of John Tobin | who departed this
life | January the 22nd 1801 | aged 58 years.

This | Stone was erected by | Redmond Barry in Memory of his Father & Mother | David Barry aged 71 | Elizabeth Barry 93 [Remainder underground.]

---

Erected | by William FitzGerald of Dongourney | in memory of his beloved mother | Johanna FitzGerald alias Downing | who departed this life Feby 17th 1828 | aged 75 years | Also his father James FitzGerald | who died June 6th 1835 | aged 77 years.

---

Erected | by Edmond Colbert of Dungourney | in memory of his beloved daughter Johanna Colbert | who died June 9th 1847 | aged 12 years.

---

Erected | by James Daly in memory of his beloved mother Johanna | FitzGerald of Dungourney who | departed this life March 24th 1831 | aged 42 years.

---

## Kilbolane Church.

[From Colonel J. Grove-White.]

' On a small tablet of modern date ' :—

```
┌─────────────────────────────────────┐
│        This is the Burial Place      │
│           of the Synans              │
│                                      │
│  (Arms.)                    1442     │
└─────────────────────────────────────┘
```

' Beneath this is a slab bearing the following inscription :—

HERE LYETH
THE BODY OF
EDMUND SYNAN
OF THE HOUSE OF
DUNERAYL FORMERLY W
HO DIED MARCH 24TH 1720
AGED 84 Y. ALSO HIS SON
JOHN SYNAN, DIED JULY
THE 25TH 1747, AGED 71 YRS
ALSO HIS WIFE, ANNE FITZ
GIBBON, OF THIS HOUSE OF
MEIN AND MILTOWN. SHE

DIED FEB. 14. 1760, AGED 91 YRS
ALSO THEIR SON, WILLIAM
SYNAN. HE DIED JAN 10, 1772
AGED 57 YEARS. THEIR
SON JAMES SYNAN DIED
MAY 1775. AGED 30 YEARS.

'The family crest, arms, and motto (Confido-in-Domino : et-non-moriemur) appear at the top of the slab, rudely carved. Burke's "General Armory" gives no Synan or Sinan coat-of-arms.'

---

## Killanully.

[From James Coleman, M.R.S.A.I.]

'This graveyard, adjoining the village of Ballygarvan, which is about midway between Cork and Carrigaline, is rather small, and stands upon a rock. Portions of the walls of the old church still remain, including the two gable ends, and the arched doorway at the south side. In the centre of the old church is the grave of a former Parish Priest, which is still evidently an object of popular devotion—a shelf having been placed in front of the headstone, which is covered with religious objects, such as small statues, with other more incongruous articles, such as an egg-cup, a feeding-bottle, a glass candlestick, a farthing, and several empty bottles. The inscription is as follows' :—

> The | Parishioners of Ballygarvan | have erected at their own Expense | to the memory of the late Rev. Florence MacCarthy | Parish Priest of Douglas and Ballygarvan who departed this life | Febry 24th 1805 | Aged 80 years.

---

'At the east end of a tall detached tomb is the following poetic epitaph' :—

Lamented Busteed what tho short thy date
Virtue not rolling Suns the mind matures
That life is long which answers Life's great end
The time that bears no fruit deserves no name
The man of Wisdom is the Man of Years.
When kindred forms have mingled into kindred dust
Congenial spirits meet to part no more
ELIZA's gone to join the early partner of her choice
To Heaven's high will submissive
Lured from a simple world disowning death's control
Her Body to earth she gave : to Christ her ransomed soul.

' There are about forty headstones here nearly all apparently of the age and pattern of those whose inscriptions have been copied as follows ' :—

### I H S

ERECTED | by JAMES LEAHY | in memory of his Father & Mother | JOHN & JANE LEAHY | Also his brother | Here lieth the remains of his two | Children Mary and James. He died April 14th 1822.

### I H S

He lieth | the body of Michael | Murly & Sister Margaret | They dep^d A D.. 1800 | and Marg^t 63 | This is the burial place | of Jn° Leahy.

### +

THE | BURIAL PLACE of | MAURICE CONNELL AND FAMILY | ERECTED | in memory of | his beloved son | MICHAEL who departed this life Nov. 10th 1840 | Aged 25 Years.

The burial place of | JEREMIAH CALLAGHAN and family of Meadstown | he departed this life | January 3rd 1829 aged 69 years.

Sacred to the Memory of MICHAEL DONEGAN | of Killingley | who died Feb^y 22nd 1847 | aged | 72 years and his beloved wife Mary | who died Feby 24th 1844.

' There is a tower-like structure in this graveyard with apparently a corbel projecting from it, which seems to have ended with a human head.'

## Marmullane Churchyard.

[From Captain R. de B. Beamish.]

' Large monument to the memory of Lieutenant Richard Roberts, R.N., " the first officer under whose command a steam vessel ever crossed the Atlantic Ocean." '

' Full text of the inscription ' :—

This stone commemorates, in the churchyard of his native parish, the merits & premature death of the first officer under whose command a steam vessel ever crossed the Atlantic Ocean. Undaunted bravery exhibited in the suppression of the slave traffic in the

African seas, a character unequalled for enterprise and
consummate skill in all the details of his profession,
recommended for this arduous service

Lieutenant Richard Roberts, R.N.

In accomplishing it he not only surpassed the wildest
visions of former days, but even the warmest anticipa-
tions of the present, gave to science triumphs she had
not dared to hope, and created an epoch for ever
memorable in the history of his country and of navigation. The thousands that shall follow in his track
must not forget who it was that first taught the world
to traverse with such marvellous rapidity that highway
of the ocean, and who in thus connecting by a voyage
of a few days duration the eastern and western hemi-
spheres, has for ever linked his name with the greatest
achievement of navigation since Columbus first revealed
Europe and America to each other.

God having permitted him this high distinction, was
pleased to decree that the leader of this great enterprise
should also be its martyr. Lieutenant Roberts perished
with all hands on board his ship the ' President ' when
on the voyage from America to Europe. She was lost
in the month of March 1841.

As the gallant seaman under whose guidance was
accomplished an undertaking the result of which
centuries will not exhaust, it is for his country—for the
world to remember him. His widow, who erects this
melancholy memorial, may be forgiven if to her even
these claims are lost in the recollection of that devoted-
ness of attachment, that uprightness and kindliness of
spirit, which for, alas ! but three brief years formed the
light and joy of her existence.

––––––

## Marshalstown Churchyard.

[From Mr. James Buckley.]

' Considerable remains of the ancient Catholic Church are still
in position. It was 28 feet 2 inches wide. The south wall is at
present 12 feet high and 45 feet long, but it was evidently much
longer originally. In this wall is a pointed doorway, in height
6 feet to apex, and in width 3 feet 6½ inches. The spring of the
arch commences 3 feet 9 inches from the ground. The doorway is
supported by a buttress at each side, and is constructed of cut
stone, chamfered; the interior is supported by a rough arch.
There is a putlog hole at each side. The wall is 2 feet 10½ inches
thick. Immediately opposite in the north wall is a somewhat
similar doorway, 2 feet 9 inches wide, and 5 feet 6 inches high.

In the south wall, to the east of the doorway, and about 4 feet from the ground, is a lancet-window, 6 inches wide, which splays internally. The dressed stone facing of this window is much displaced and ready to fall, but for a growth of ivy which keeps it together. These ruins, if cleared of the growth of wood that infests them, could with very little outlay be made very sightly and interesting for many years to come. One of the neatest Protestant churches in Ireland stands in this churchyard.

'It was built at the expense of one of the Earls of Kingston, and Divine Service is held in it on Sundays by our fellow-member, the Very Rev. Canon Moore.

'The following is a copy of the oldest inscription here':—

+

IHS

HERE LYETH YE
BODY OF MICH
AEL MOLAHANE
WHO DEPARTED
THIS LIFE MARCH
YE 30TH 1728

## Passage West Churchyard.

[From Captain R. de B. Beamish.]

'Inscription on the tomb of Edward Daniel Brown':—

Erected
by
William and Anne Brown
Of
Mount Prospect
To the memory of their only and dearly beloved son
Edward Daniel Brown
who
Full of hope and in the morning of manhood
Was suddenly called into Eternity
By accidental drowning in this Harbour
On Thursday July 23rd 1857
In the 20th year of his age.
In him were combined
High intellectual attainments
Manliness of character, integrity of purpose
And Kindliness of feeling.
As the
Benefactor of the poor, the friend of all, the enemy of none
His memory
Will ever be cherished in this neighbourhood.

**THE BROWN MONUMENT IN THE CHURCHYARD OF
PASSAGE WEST, CO. CORK.**

[*From a photograph supplied by Captain R. de B. Beamish.*]

More especially by those,
Who found him
A dutiful and affectionate son, a fond brother, an unwavering friend.
In whose many virtues and heart cherished memories
This tablet has been inscribed,
As a last sad tribute
To departed worth.

Because God loved him
He whispered to the stormy winds
And to the angry waves
Take him to his home.

## Marmullane Churchyard.

[From Lord Walter FitzGerald.]

' This churchyard is situated on the summit of the high ground above Passage West, overlooking the river Lee, and its expansion called Lough Mahon.

' There is no trace of the ancient church, and the burial-ground contains no tombs of any antiquity, with the exception of one slab, which was brought to my notice by the Rev. C. A. Webster, Rector of Passage West, who has kindly supplied the photograph here reproduced, and to whom the discovery of the slab is due.    Writing

in the month of April, 1911, Mr. Webster states that "it is about thirteen years since I first saw the stone, but it was afterwards covered over, and the grass allowed to grow on it. When I went to look for it some time ago it was well under the earth, and only for the exertions of my parishioner, who now resides in the old Glebe house, I fear it would have fared badly."

'The position of the slab is about the middle of the churchyard. It lies flat, though to be photographed it was temporarily placed upright.

'The inscription is not complete, as the date does not appear to have ever been cut on the slab. The lettering is partly in "the black letter" and partly in Roman capitals, raised and rudely cut. Unfortunately the Christian name of the deceased's father is beyond deciphering. Mr. M. J. M'Enery, of the Dublin Record Office, is of the opinion that the inscription should be read':—

> Hic iacet Phillippus filius . . . . . Ronane de Corck qui obiit Pesti [l] enciæ, anno doii [domini] . .

'It will be noticed in the rubbing on the opposite page that the *l* in *pestilenciæ* has been omitted by the stone-cutter.

Judging by the lettering, the date of this monument may be the end of the sixteenth or commencement of the seventeenth century.

## COUNTY DONEGAL.

[Nil.]

## COUNTY DOWN.

### Banbridge Church, Parish of Seapatrick.

[From the Ven. E. D. Atkinson, Archdeacon of Dromore.]

'A white marble tablet set on gray marble; sculptured icebergs with a wreck appear above the following inscription, below which is a bust':—

> FAR FROM THIS SPOT | IN SOME UNKNOWN, BUT NOT UNHONOURED, RESTING-PLACE, LIE ALL THAT WAS MORTAL OF | FRANCIS RAWDON MOIRA CROZIER, CAPT^N R.N. | 5^TH SON OF THE LATE GEORGE CROZIER, ESQ^R. | HE WAS BORN SEPTEMBER 1796, ENTERED THE ROYAL NAVY JUNE 1810, AND SERVED WITH HIGH DISTINCTION | IN SEVERAL EXPLORING VOYAGES UNDER SIR E. PARRY, AND WITH SIR J. C. ROSS IN THE ARCTIC AND ANTARCTIC REGIONS. | HE LEFT ENGLAND MAY 1845 IN COMMAND OF H.M.S. TERROR, WITH

THE RONANE SLAB IN THE MARMULLANE

SIR J. FRANKLIN OF H.M.S. EREBUS | IN THE EXPEDITION
FOR THE DISCOVERY OF THE N.WEST PASSAGE. | FROM THIS
HEROIC SERVICE NEITHER HE NOR ANY OF HIS BRAVE COM-
PANIONS EVER RETURNED. | HIS UNBENDING INTEGRITY &
TRUTHFULNESS COMBINED WITH EXTREME AMIABILITY WON
THE ESTEEM | AND LOVE OF ALL WHO KNEW HIM. THE
FAITH THAT INFLUENCED HIS LIFE IS NOW A SOURCE OF |
TRUEST CONSOLATION TO HIS SORROWING FRIENDS.

This Tablet has been Erected | in his Native Place by
his | surviving brothers and sisters | in heartfelt and
affectionate | testimony to his fraternal | love and
Christian character.
If I take the wings of the | morning, and dwell in the
uttermost part of the | sea even there shall thy | hand
lead me. Ps. 139. 9.
Them also which sleep | in Jesus, will God bring | with
him. I Thess. IV.
R. KIRK, R.H.A., Sculptor.

---

## Banbridge Presbyterian Church, Down-shire Road.

[From Captain R. Linn, Christchurch, New Zealand.]

' Marble tablet in body of church ' :—

IN MEMORY OF
THE REV. JOHN MONTGOMERY,
WHO WAS FOR NEARLY 20 YEARS
THE MINISTER OF THE CONGREGATION
STATEDLY ASSEMBLED WITHIN THESE WALLS,
AND WHOSE FIDELITY AS A MINISTER OF CHRISTS GOSPEL
COMBINED WITH PURITY OF LIFE UNSPOTTED INTEGRITY
AND ENLARGED CHRISTIAN CHARITY
COMMANDED UNIVERSAL RESPECT.
THIS MONUMENT IS ERECTED
BY THE MEMBERS OF THE FLOCK WHICH SO LONG ENJOYED
THE BENEFIT OF HIS ZEALOUS ABLE AND IMPRESSIVE
MINISTRATIONS.
BORN 21ST MARCH 1819, ORDAINED AT LIMAVADY OCT 8TH 1840
INSTALLED AT BANBRIDGE 15 DEC —— DIED 28TH APRIL 1867.

---

A memorial | of esteem and regard of the | Presby-
terian Congregation of Banbridge, | To their late
Pastor, | The Rev. Nathaniel Shaw. | A man, distin-
guished in public and private life, by an unbending
integrity of principle, and | an undeviating adherence

to truth. | His house was the asylum of the unfortunate, and the seat of unaffected hospitality. | Whilst his heart embraced the human kind, his particular friendships were warm, generous, and active. Convinced of the importance of Christianity, he laboured in | its cause with ability, zeal, and effect. | He died on the 3<sup>rd</sup> of July, in the year of our Lord 1812, in the 53<sup>rd</sup> year of his age, and | the 23<sup>rd</sup> of His ministry.

## Clonmallon (Warrenpoint) Old Churchyard.

[From Capt. R. Lunn, New Zealand.]

Here lys John Henry | who departed in y<sup>e</sup> year of God 1687.

Here lyeth y<sup>e</sup> body of | John Lillburn | who departed this life | January 13<sup>th</sup> in the year of our Lord | 1724.

Here lyeth the body | of William Ormondy who | died May y<sup>e</sup> 20<sup>th</sup> 1734.

In memory of | Captain Peachey Sowerby | of White-haven, who died 26 April 1792 | aged 33 years.

Erected in memory of | Thomas M<sup>c</sup>Ateer | of Warren-point, who departed | this life November 23<sup>rd</sup> 1814 | aged 27 years | may he rest in peace.

Sacred | to the memory of Catherine relict | of the Right Honourable William Brownlow | of Lurgan, Co. Armagh | and daughter of Roger Hall Esq<sup>r</sup> | of Narrow-Water | who departed this life | on the 27<sup>th</sup> of April 1824.

## Donaghadee.

[From Messrs. Francis C. and Philip Crossle.]

(Continued from p. 41.)

SACRED
To the memory of
WILLIAM LOWRY OF BALLYNOE
who departed this life on the first of May 1780.
Aged 96 years.

ALSO
To the Memory of his Wife
JANE LOWRY alias LOWDEN
who died on the 24<sup>th</sup> of June, 1790 Aged 87 Years.
LIKEWISE
To the Memory of their Son
MURRAY LOWRY
who departed this life on the first of March, 1805.
Aged 60 Years.
ALSO
To the Memory of his Wife
ELEANOR LOWRY alias CASEMENT
who departed this life on the first of Nov'r 1818.
Aged 73 Years.
AND
To the Memory of their Son
Sir THOMAS LOWRY, C.B. of the Honourable East
India Company's Service, and Major in the seventh
Native Infantry, who after 23 years of active and
Distinguished service in India
DIED
at Burchampoor in the province of Bengal on the
2<sup>nd</sup> December, 1819.  Aged 39 Years.

———

SACRED
To the Memory of
HUGH M<sup>c</sup>CONNELL LOWRY
who departed this life on the 27<sup>th</sup> October, 1827
Aged 24 Years
he was Son to JAMES LOWRY Esq<sup>r</sup> of Bally-
maconnell, and, Nephew to Sir THOMAS LOWRY
late MAJOR in the BENGAL Establishment.
Also the Memory of his Brother
THOMAS CASEMENT LOWRY, Solicitor
who departed this life on the 20<sup>th</sup> April 1831
In the 22<sup>nd</sup> Year of his age
Also to the Memory of their Sister
ELEANOR JANE LOWRY,
who departed this life in the Bloom of youth
on the 8<sup>th</sup> March, 1832, Aged 21 years.
Also their Sister ELIZABETH died Aged 2 years
ALSO
Here resteth in GOD the mortal remains of
MARY LOWRY alias M<sup>c</sup>CONNELL their Mother
who departed this life on the 23<sup>rd</sup> Sept. 1833
Aged 49 Years.
Blessed are the dead which die in the Lord

Also her Son JAMES LOWRY
of Ballymaconnell, who departed this life
on the 5<sup>th</sup> December 1861 aged 41 years
Also to the memory of William Clarke Lowry
son of the late James Lowry, who departed this
life on the 13<sup>th</sup> January, 1881, Aged 26 years.
ELIZA KNOX, wife of the above
JAMES LOWRY, who departed this life
on the 8<sup>th</sup> March 1899 Aged 73 Years.
Also CHARLES CASEMENT LOWRY, who
departed this life in the year 1838 Aged 20 Years.

' These two preceding stones are in a railed-in enclosure.'

———

Here lyeth y<sup>e</sup> Body
of : james LOWREY · who
DEPARTED this life : MARCH
y<sup>e</sup> 14<sup>th</sup> 1733⁴ Aged 77 years
Alſo his wife MARY cane
who DIED · MARCH y<sup>e</sup> 15<sup>th</sup> 1733⁴
Aged 75 years both in one GRAVE
Also the Body of Mary Lowry
who departed this Life the
20<sup>th</sup> of June 1756 Aged 26
Years.

———

THIS
Is James Smyth's, Burial Place
Here Lieth the Body of Jane
Smyth his wife who Died Nov. 26<sup>th</sup>
1806 : Æ 63 Yr<sup>s</sup> ⁓ Alſo 3 of her
Children who Died Young
Alſo James Smyth, who departed
this life July 10<sup>th</sup> 1822. aged 88
Years.

———

Here lieth the body of Elisabeth
Tanner, alias Maxwell wife to patrick
Tanner, who departed this life Sep<sup>t</sup>
the 23<sup>d</sup> 1812 Aged 53 years.
This stone is inscribed by HUGH TANNER of
Ballyhay in remembrance of his beloved children
viz. SUSANNA MARIA, who departed this life
on the 9<sup>th</sup> day of April A.D. 1851. Aged 3 years.
Likewise his Son DAVID HUGH, who also departed
this life on the 11<sup>th</sup> day of April A.D. 1851
Aged 7 Years.

William Tanner's
Burying ground
D-DEE
' Upright freestone headstone.'

---

Erected
by
Robert Tanner of Donaghadee, in
Memory of his Father Hugh Tanner
Who departed this life 13ᵗʰ January
1839 Aged 64 years.
Also John, son of the above-named Robert Tanner
who departed this life 25ᵗʰ June 1848, Aged
8 years.
Also Margaret Daughter to the said Robert
Tanner who died 2ⁿᵈ Decʳ 1855, Aged 12 Years.
Also Eliza Daughter to the above Robert
Tanner who died 26ᵗʰ June 1863 Æ 25 years
Also Ann Wife to the above Hugh Tanner
who died 15ᵗʰ April 1861, Aged 91 Years.
Also the above named Robert Tanner
who died 15th June 1871.   Aged 73 years.

---

Here Lyeth
The Body of Iamef Tanner
who died Feb. 27ᵗʰ 1724 Aged
66 Years.   Also here lieth
the body of James Tanner
. . . . . . who departed
. . . . . . A.D. 1825
' Rest of inscription buried.'

---

This is Wᵐ Tanner's Burying Place wherein is Interred
his Wife Margᵗ MᶜCredy, who depᵗᵈ this Life July 17.
1792. Æ 54 Yrˢ Also the above William Tanner who
departed this life 23ᵈ April 1811.  Aged 70 years.  This
stone is inscribed by William, the second son to the
memory of his father John Tanner, who departed this
life on the 22ⁿᵈ day of March, A.D. 1830 in the 62ⁿᵈ
year of his age.

*(To be continued.)*

## Downpatrick Cathedral.

[From W. Harris's " History of the County Down, 1744."]

' On page 34 ' :—

" On the rising ground, at the entrance to this town, formerly stood a noble house of the Right Honourable Edward Lord Cromwell, burned down by the Irish rebels in 1641.

" This Gentleman came over into Ireland in the reign of King James I, and was Captain of an Independent Troop at Down, where he built this House, some of the ruins whereof yet appear, and in which he lived with great hospitality and credit. He was descended from Lord Cromwell, Earl of Essex, in the reign of King Henry VIII, and enjoyed from him an estate in Devonshire, which he exchanged with Blount, Lord Viscount Mountjoy, for the Abbey lands of Down, Inis, and Saul, granted to that nobleman for his great services to the Crown. He died here, and was buried in the middle of the old Cathedral, near the east end, and on his gravestone is this inscription " :—

HERE LIETH INTERRED THE BODY OF THE RIGHT HONOURABLE EDWARD GROMWELL BARON OF OKEHAM. DECEASED 24TH OF SEPTEMBER 1607· ALSO THE BODY OF THE HONOURABLE OLIVER GROMWELL, SON TO THE RIGHT HONOURABLE THOMAS, EARL OF ARDGLASS, AND GRANDSON OF THE SAID EDWARD, DECEASED 19TH OF OCTOBER 1668·

' The following extracts from Burke's " Extinct Peerage " give the descent of the members of the Cromwell family named on the tombstone ' :—

" Thomas Cromwell, son of Walter Cromwell, a blacksmith at Putney, upon his return from foreign service, under the Duke of Bourbon, obtained a situation in the suite of Cardinal Wolsey and, after the fall of that celebrated Prelate, was taken into the service of King Henry VIII, in which he evinced so much zeal and ability that he was promoted to some of the most important offices of the State. On the 9th July, 1536, he was created Baron Cromwell of Okeham (in Rutlandshire), and on the 10th April, 1589, Earl of Essex. But his elevation was not more rapid than his decline. His instrumentality in allying the king with Anne of Cleves proved his downfall, and on the 24th July, 1540, he was beheaded ; but his son Gregory, who in his lifetime had been summoned to Parliament as Lord Cromwell, had that dignity confirmed to him by Letters Patent in the December following his father's execution.

[From a brother-in-law of Thomas Cromwell, Earl of Essex, named Morgan Williams, whose son and heir assumed the name of Cromwell, was descended Oliver Cromwell the Lord Protector.]

"Gregory Cromwell, Baron Cromwell of Okeham, died in 1551, and was succeeded by his eldest son Henry.

"Henry, 2nd Baron, died in 1592, leaving by his wife Mary Paulet, daughter of John, 2nd Marquis of Winchester, a son and heir Edward, the individual named on the tombstone.

"Edward, 3rd Baron Cromwell, of Okeham, took to his second wife Frances, daughter of William Rugge, of Norfolk, by whom he had Thomas his successor.

"Thomas, 4th Baron Cromwell, of Okeham, was created on the 22nd November, 1624, Viscount Lecale, and on the 15th April, 1645, Earl of Ardglass. He married Elizabeth, daughter and heiress of Robert Meverell, of Throwleigh, in Staffordshire, by whom he had several children, the third son being the Oliver Cromwell named on the tomb. His father, Lord Ardglass, died in 1653. The title became extinct on the death of the 7th Baron and 4th Earl in 1687."

W. Fitz G.

## Drumballyroney.

[From Captain R. Linn, New Zealand.]

This stone was fixed by the | Rev. Hugh O'Kelly | priest of Down in memory of his | father brothers and sisters | who lie here | viz.:—Teague O'Kelly of Crobane | departed in yᵉ year of God 1725 aged 49 | the two sisters aged 15 | Daniel in yᵉ year 1737 Neal year 1741 | aged 22 | Hugh Teague and Nelly Patt O'Kelly's children of Crossan | son to Teague of Crobane.

John Hill | merchant of Rathfriland | 1726 | His wife Isabella Knox 1724.

Here lyeth yᵉ body of | Mʳˢ Isabella Moor | . . . who departed this | life yᵉ 7 July 1726 age 62 | years also Here lyeth | the body of Francis Moor.

H. Reilly 1747.

William Bradford of Cavan | 29 November 1770 aged 64.

Erected by | Joseph May | Physician Ballybrick and Rathfriland | Samuel May died 1770 | Joseph May died 1830 | Samuel May died 1869.

---

Robert Kirk | 1771.

---

Here lyeth the body of | Aily Doyle | Departed February 20th 1783 | aged 23.

---

Here lyeth the body of | Arthur Doyle | who departed this life June 11th 1783 | aged 52 years.

---

Mr James Hilles | 1785.

---

Mr Martin Hilles 18 July | 1800.

---

Here lys the body of | Neil Kelly | who departed this life February | 22nd 1787 | aged 67 | also his wife Mable Mooney.

---

William Strain | 17 May 1792.

---

Eliza Swan 1792.

---

George Scott of Tullyquilly | died 18 April 1800.

---

Samuel Tuffts | 1814.

---

Stephen Lennon | who died 1818.

---

Michael Corbitt of Lisnacreevy | 1823.

---

Bryan Doran of Rathfriland.

---

Robert McMullan.

---

'In a note Mr. Digenan says that " these last two tombstones seem to be very old, but there is no date on either of them. The latter is a large horizontal red sandstone, and bears the arms of the MacMullans, who were an important family in the district in former times."

'The MacMullan family gave to the Catholic Church many clerics, some of them of eminence. Some members of this family conformed in the early part of the eighteenth century, who, in later years, gave to the Protestant Churches men of standing and ability. Colonel Daniel Magennis raised a regiment of Dragoons in Down for service under James II; amongst the officers were two MacMullans. O'Laverty in his "Diocese of Down and Connor" (vol, i, p. 313) says: "The common ancestor of this family was named Shane Mor MacMullan, whose descendants were located in Clonduff, Drumgooland, and Kinalarty. General S. F. MacMullan, of the Indian Army, who died in 1896, aged eighty-four, was a member of this family.

'Drumballyroney burial-ground was the principal burial-place of the chiefs of the Magennis family. Sir Arthur Magennis, the first Viscount Magennis, of Iveagh, was interred here on the 15th June, 1629, and probably the second Viscount also. Many other chiefs of this family must be buried in Drumballyroney, though not a single monument bears the name of Magennis.'

---

## Drumbeg Churchyard.

[From Mr. W. F. Reynolds.]

'Flat stone':—

Here is interred the body of the undernamed John Feryes of . . . who departed this life the 30 of Octob^r 1708 . . . 74 years of . . . Here is interred the body of Ales, wife to John Feris of Dunnury, (Dunmurry) who deceased November the 18, 1691, aged 63 years. Also Ales thare davghter deceased November the . . 1679 aged 16 years.

---

Here lyeth the body of John Harrison who died the 14^th of June 1740 aged 49 years. Also his wife, Rachael Harrison, alias Boyd, who died the 10^th of August 1736 aged 30 years.
Here lyeth the body of James Harison who departed this life the 9 day of December 1734 aged 9 years.

---

'Upright stone':—

Here lyeth the remains of James Kennedy, son of James Trail Kennedy, of Belfast, who departed this life, at Windsor, on the 29^th Dec 1806, aged 14 years.

' Upright stone ' :—

Here lyeth the body of Patrick Hart who departed this
life November the 1- 1756 aged 70 years.

———

' Monumental pillar having rectangular base, about four
feet high, on front side of which a marble tablet is inserted
bearing the inscription. On the base is erected a similar, but
narrower, column. On this, surrounded by an ornamental oval,
the arms sketched are cut in marble. The crest stands clear of
the surface, and is so weather-worn that identification of the
animal represented is difficult. A short obelisk on top of all com-
pletes the monument ' :—

In memory of John Younghusband of Ballydrain Esq<sup>r</sup>
who died 10<sup>th</sup> April 1843 in his 89<sup>th</sup> year and also of his
wife Letitia, daughter of George Black of Stranmillis
Esq<sup>r</sup> and widow of William Harrison Esq<sup>r</sup> of Belfast
who died 17<sup>th</sup> Sept<sup>r</sup> 1833 in her 79<sup>th</sup> year.

———

' Flat stone ' :—

Erected by Sam<sup>l</sup> Law of Banbridge in memory of his
sister, Mary Ann, who departed this life 7<sup>th</sup> June 1808
aged 17 years.

———

' Flat stone ' : —

Here lyeth the body of William Brice who deceased the
26 of Aprill 1696, and Arthur, his son, deceased in
March 1691 : and the body of Jane Brice, alias Kelso,
his wyfe who deceased October the 12 1697 and
William ther son deceased in Jenuar 96.

' Flat stone ' :—

> Here lyeth the body of Archibald Hamilton who de-
> parted the 9<sup>th</sup> of February 1725 aged 80 years : also
> Margaret, his wife, sister of the late Arthur Maxwell
> of Drum, Esq<sup>r</sup>, who died the 12<sup>th</sup> of Janr<sup>y</sup> 1736 aged
> 85 years.

' The above grave is surrounded by an iron railing, which
encloses also a raised tomb. The lettered flat slab on top of this is
broken in pieces, parts being missing. Almost the whole of the
inscription, however, exists.'

> Here are interred the bodys of James Maxwell of Drum
> Esq<sup>r</sup> the 20<sup>th</sup> of March 1681 aged 70 years. Also Ann,
> his wife, the 30<sup>th</sup> of March 1684 aged 70 years and
> Arthur Maxwell of Drum Esq<sup>r</sup>, their son, the 22<sup>nd</sup> of
> January 1720 aged 74 years : also Letitia the wife of
> James Hamilton Maxwell, Esq<sup>r</sup> November the 17<sup>th</sup>
> 1740 aged 55 years : and also the above named James
> Hamilton . . axwell of Drum Esq<sup>r</sup> . . the 21<sup>st</sup>
> February 1751 in the . . . . r of his age.

' Underneath the above inscription the following arms are
sculptured ' :—

## Drumbeg Church.

' Tablet on front side of buttress of church tower ' :—

> Near this lies interred the body of Alexander George
> Stewart of Windsor and Macedon, Esq, who died the
> 10<sup>th</sup> of January 1796 aged 59 years : also of Miss
> Elinor Stewart, his sister, of Windsor who died the
> 20<sup>th</sup> of March 1806 aged 80 years and likewise of
> Thomas Stewart, Esq. of Whitehouse who died at
> Windsor the 29<sup>th</sup> of March 1806 aged 78 years.

To the memory of Jane Stewart, daughter of William Hogg of Malone and wife to John Stewart of Ballydrain, who departed this life the 17th day of March 1778, aged 80 years : also her daughter, Martha, wife of Israel Younghusband, who died 7th December 1758 aged 27 years. Also to the memory of John Stewart of Ballydrain, husband of the above Jane, who died 10th Aprile 1784, aged 83 yr[s].

—Hem Quanto minus Est cum Reliquis Versan quam cui Meminisse—Also here lies interred Mary Isabella, wife to Robert Stewart of Ballydrain, who died 6th of December 1785, aged 35 yr[s] and also John Stewart, aged 11 yr[s], son to the above Robert and Mary. Also the body of Robert Stewart of Ballydrain, who died Jan[y] the 9th 1797, aged 55 years : also the body of his son George Alex[r]. Stewart who died Nov[r] 1805, aged 27 years, leaving two sons who died abroad early in life.

' Arms—A fesse chequy, over all a bend engrailed.
' Crest—On a wreath a dexter hand couped at the wrist holding a human heart.
' Motto—" Sola Juvat Virtus." '

———

' At back of tower ' :—

Here lyeth the body of Anna Willson, Daughter to John Wilson, laird of Crogline, wife to John Stewart of Bellidraine, who departed this life the 25 of December 1682 aged 63 years. Here also is laied the body of John Stewart above mentioned who died Nov the 4, 1691 in his 70 year and alsoe the body of Thom[s] Stewart their son who deceased the 11 of July 1715 aged 55 years and of his daughter Ana Stewart who deceased the 8 of June 1707 aged 2 years and of his daughter Margaret Stewart who deceased the 19 of June 1708 aged 6 years.

———

' Close to above ' :—

Here lyeth the body of A . . Wilson, daughter to the laird of Croglain, wife to John Stewart of Ballydraine, who departed this life Dec[m] 25 1682, aged 63. Here also is laid the body of Jn[o] Stewart who departed this life Nov 4, 1691 in his 70th year : his father, Capt[n] Will[m] Stewart, son of Lord Garlie, was killed at Kilcullen Bridge, he and his escort cut all to pieces by a party of Roman Catholics in 1641.

Here also is laid the body of Thomas Stewart who departed this life the 11<sup>th</sup> of July 1715, aged 55, and his daughters, Anna and Margaret, one 2 years old, the other 6. His wife, Martha, died abroad 1755. George, the son of Tho<sup>s</sup>, who was lost at sea 1745. Here also lieth the body of Martha Stewart, wife of Mr. Younghusband who departed this life the 7 of December 1758, aged 27. [Two or three more lines illegible.]

---

' Close to the above ' :—

Here lyeth the body of Thomas Martin, Marchant, Belfast, who departed this life the 29 of October Anno Dom 1685 aged 42 years ; also the body of Flora Stewart, his wife, daughter to John Stewart of Balydraine, who departed this life the 27 of April Anno Dom 1683 aged 28 years. Here lyeth the body of Jane Stewart who departed Sept 11<sup>th</sup> 1734 aged 66 years : also her husband, George Stewart, brother of the above Flora Martin and son of the late John Stewart of Ballydrain who departed July 20<sup>th</sup> 1740 aged 74 years : also Elizabeth Stewart, daughter of the above George Stewart, who departed Sep<sup>t</sup> 24<sup>th</sup> 1777 aged 72 years.

---

' Flat stone in churchyard ' :—

Here lyeth the body of Frances (*sic*) Tornly, twin son of Joshua Tornly of Mallon, who departed this life the 1 day of March 1699, of age 30 years. And the body of Singo Tornly who departed this life the 14 of February 1709, of age 36 years. And the body of Edward Tornly who departed this life Mar 18, 1732, aged 53 years.

---

## Drumgath Graveyard.

[From Captain R. Linn, New Zealand.]

Pray for y<sup>e</sup> Rev<sup>d</sup> Father | Manus Fegan, Parish Priest of the Parish of Clonallon | who constantly taught his flock | by word and example | Died March 8<sup>th</sup> 1726 | aged 74 years.

[NOTE.—Manus Fegan, of Clonallon, appears on the list of King James's adherents who were attainted at Banbridge in 1691.]

---

Here lieth the body of | Patrick Magennis | who departed this life | 1747.

Here lieth the body of | Rose Magin | wife of Charles M<sup>c</sup>Convel who | departed this life the | 6<sup>th</sup> day of July 1736.

---

Here lies the body of | Cornellis Kerney | who departed this life | on the 10<sup>th</sup> of January in the year of our Lord | 1767 aged 80 years also his wife | Mary Kerney | who departed this life November 10<sup>th</sup> 1791 | aged 84 years | also Daniel Kerney.

---

Here lyeth the body of | John Fegan | son of Francis Fegan of Barinmeen | who departed this life May the 7<sup>th</sup> 1776 | aged 28 years.

---

Here lieth the body of | Terence Doyle | who departed this life December | 1777.

---

Here lieth the body of | Henry FitzPatrick | who died June 1777 | aged 24 years.

---

Here lies the body of | Arthur M<sup>c</sup>Convill | of Bavin who died March 4<sup>th</sup> 1777 | aged 77 years.

---

Here lyeth the body of | Francis Poland | who departed this life November 23<sup>rd</sup> 1777 | aged 80.

Daniel Fitzpatrick of Cleomack | A.D. 1780.

---

Here lies the body of | Patrick Keenin who died May 12<sup>th</sup> 1782 | aged 76 years.

---

Here lies the body of | Patrick Ferin | who died 1782. aged 76 years.

---

This is the burying-ground of | Terence M<sup>c</sup>Manus of Benagh | who departed this life March 2<sup>nd</sup> 1790 | aged 66 years.

---

Here lieth the body of | Hugh Fegan | of Barnmeen who departed this life | 1790 aged 41 years.

Here lieth the body of | Hugh M<sup>c</sup>Convill | of Drumgreenagh, who died 1795 | aged 69.

———

Here lieth the body of | Daniel M<sup>c</sup>Cann | who died 11<sup>th</sup> May in the year of | our Lord 1795.

———

This stone was erected by | Bryan FitzPatrick | of Ballygorianmore in memory | of his father Matthew FitzPatrick | and also of his mother Eliza | and brothers and sisters. [No date.]

———

Here lieth the remains of | Michael M<sup>c</sup>Convel | who departed this life August 1<sup>st</sup> 1813 | aged 30 years also his mother Alice | M<sup>c</sup>Convel who departed this life | June 28<sup>th</sup> 1806 | aged 46 years.

———

Hugh Breen | was interred here 1810 also Daniel Breen | his son who departed 11<sup>th</sup> August 1811 | aged 31 years.

———

Erected to the memory of | Patrick Morgan | of Carneny who died | December 23<sup>rd</sup> 1810 | aged 80 years also his wife Allas | who departed April 12<sup>th</sup> 1822 | aged 80 years.

———

Here lieth the body of | Hugh Toman | of Rathfriland who departed | this life March 27<sup>th</sup> 1829 | aged 21 years.

———

Here lies the body of | John M<sup>c</sup>Convill | of Drumgreenagh who departed | this life March 7<sup>th</sup> 1822 | aged 84 years | also his son James M<sup>c</sup>Convill.

———

Here lieth the body of | Robert Hanna | of Bavin who died January 1825 | aged 70.

———

Mark M<sup>c</sup>Clorey | of Ballydullaney departed this life | 27<sup>th</sup> March 1829 | This stone was erected by his son, Henry.

### Holywood Churchyard.

[Contributed by Mr. T. U. Sadleir, from Mason's " Parochia Survey, 1814," vol. iii, p. 199.]

Here lie the remains of
The Hon. Robert Seymour Nugent
Son of the Earl of Westmeath, and Elizabeth his wife
Who departed this life on the
12ᵗʰ day of July 1810 aged five years.
Short was thy span, sweet babe, prescribed the years
Which closed thy journey through this vale of tears
If feeling, more than common in a child,
If patience, suffering borne wlth temper mild,
Could resignation in the hour of death,
Could virtue's self have stayed thy fleeting breath,
Thy life hath yet been spared ; thy friends no more
In tearful accents would thy loss deplore :
Yet why deplore for thee, why longer grieve
For thee, who now, in realms of bliss dost live,
Who, in thy Saviour's bosom dost recline,
The blest retreat of innocence like thine !

———

Burial place of the Revᵈ James Hamilton of Mᵗ Collier; erected at the desire of his widow, who " enjoined that ostentation should be avoided, as but ill according with the meek character of him to whom it stands dedicated."

———

' An ancient tombstone, date illegible, bearing the name " Russell, of Holywood," aged 118.

———

### Kilbroney (Rostrevor) Old Churchyard.

[From Captain R. Linn, Christchurch, New Zealand.]

' I have compiled the following inscriptions from a paper contributed by Mr. Hugh Digenan to a local newspaper on " The Ancient Graveyards of South Down." Most of the inscriptions were copied many years ago, and it is likely that not a few of them could not now be read ' :—

Memento Mori | Here lyeth the body of Adam Crelly | who dyed the 9ᵗʰ day of December 1713 | in the 12ᵗʰ year of his age.

Here lieth the body of | Mary **Flannegan** | who departed this life | June yᵉ 29ᵗʰ 1744.

---

Here lyeth the body of | Alice Hanlon | wife of Captain Felix Hanlon | of Rostrevor who departed this life | April 16ᵗʰ 1760 | aged 76 years.

---

Memento Mori | Here lyeth the body of Mary Fegan | who departed this life | June the 14ᵗʰ 1760 aged 83 years.

---

Edward Kielty, 1775.

---

This is the burying-place | of Thomas and Patrick Feran of Narrow-Water | 1779.

---

Here lyeth the body of | Bryan Feran | who departed this life | February 12ᵗʰ 1780 aged 66 years | also Cherry Feran who | departed this life August 15ᵗʰ 1787 | aged 21 years.

---

Here lyeth the body of | John O'Neill | who departed this life 16ᵗʰ May 1790 | aged 66 years.
[This stone bears the proud symbol of the Red Hand.]

---

Here lyeth the body of | Arthur Maginnes who departed this life the 19 August, 1802 | aged 81 years.

---

### illyleagh Old Churchyard (opposite Hamilton's Castle).

[From Mr. William F. Reynolds.]

Here lyeth the bodeys of VIII children sons & daughters vnt° John Stewart of Ballymurren.

| | |
|---|---|
| Patricke Stewart obyt | 10ᵗʰ Octʳ 1628. |
| Thomas | the 14ᵗʰ Jvne 1631. |
| Marion | the 24ᵗʰ Julye 1631. |
| Robert | 27 Decemʳ 1634. |
| Ludowicke | 30 Decemʳ 1635. |
| Grissel | 11 Avgvsᵗ 1638. |
| Anthony | 24 Octʳ 1641. |

John the eldest son died the 13 of Avgvst 1642. Also the body of Joanna Stewart Graham, the wife of Captain John Alexander Graham Grand Grand Daughter of the late John Stewart of Ballymoran who died at Antrim on the 7ᵗʰ day of February 1801 aged 26 years.

## Kilmore Churchyard.

[From Mr. William F. Reynolds.]

' On tablet over entrance door in gable of vault ' :—

The burying place of the Pottingers since 1602 being destroyed by the building of the Church in Belfast in 1813 part of the old tomb was removed here out of respect to the memory of Charlotte Pottinger whose remains lie in the adjoining grave.

# COUNTY DUBLIN.

## Balbriggan Church.

[From Miss Hillas.]

' Mural tablets ' :—

The Honourable George Hamilton of Hampton | in the County of Dublin | Third Baron of His Majesty's Court of Exchequer | in Ireland | departed this life on the 14th day of November 1793 | in the 63rd year of his age | He was a man true to his God and to the religion which | he professed ; full of affection to his brethren of mankind, | faithful to his friends, generous to his enemies, warm with | compassion to the unfortunate ; self-denying to little private | interests and pleasures, but zealous for public interest and | happiness ; magnanimous without being proud, humble without | being mean ; just without being harsh ; simple in his manners | but manly in his feelings ; on whose word you could entirely | rely ; whose countenance never deceived you ; whose professions | of kindness were the effusion of the heart, in him Ireland | lost a powerful supporter of her trade and manufactures | and his tenantry the most benevolent of landlords | He married Elizabeth Hamilton daughter to | George Hamilton Esq of Tyrella in the County of Down | a lady endowed with every virtue that could make her | worthy of a husband whom she so truly loved and revered. | This monument is erected by | the Reverend George Hamilton of Hampton | to recall the affectionate regret | with which he cherishes the memory of such parents | and to hold them out to the imitation of his children | as examples of the highest public and private virtues.

In memory of | a beloved husband and father | the Rev<sup>d</sup> George Hamilton of Hampton Hall | who departed this life on 1<sup>st</sup> of March A.D. 1833 | in the 64<sup>th</sup> year of his age | and whose mortal remains are deposited in a vault beneath. | This monument has been erected by his attached widow Anna Hamilton | and his grateful and most affectionate children | George Alexander Hamilton | late M.P. for the City and now M.P. for the University of Dublin | Thomas Claude George Hamilton, and Harriet Swan | Eminent like his father, the Hon<sup>ble</sup> Baron Hamilton | for the highest public and private virtues, his path | through life was one of continued and active usefulness | beloved by all who knew him | he . . . bore . . . towards . . . all those kindly feelings which | are the marks and fruits of a Christian spirit | he saw Death coming, but to him there was nothing awful in its approach | for he was enabled to regard it not as a king of terrors | but as a messenger of peace and joy | while with his latest accents | he bore testimony to the truth of God's Word | that all have sinned, he bore testimony also to the truth of those glad tidings | and their application to himself that through the merits | and sufferings of his Redeemer and Lord an atonement | had been made sufficient for the salvation of all. | Our beloved mother, the above named Anna Hamilton | who was daughter of Thomas Pepper Esq. of Ballygarth Castle | died at Hampton Hall on the 8th Feb 1849 aged 72 | after a life of the most active Christian benevolence | in the full assurance of salvation | through our Lord and Saviour Jesus Christ | her remains are deposited in the family vault underneath this church.

---

The Right Honorable | George Alexander Hamilton | of Hampton Hall in the County of Dublin, D.L. L.L.D. | whose remains rest in a vault beneath this church | was the eldest son of | the Rev<sup>d</sup> George Hamilton | He was born at Tyrella, Co. Down, on the 29<sup>th</sup> August 1801 | and educated at Rugby and Trinity College, Oxford | He represented the City of Dublin in Parliament in 1836 | and 1837 and the University of Dublin from 1843 to 1859 | He was twice Financial Secretary and during twelve years | Parliament Secretary to the Treasury and afterwards | a Commissioner of Church Temporalities in Ireland. | Inflexible integrity and stainless honour characterized | his public career;

throughout which from youth to age | he sought to promote the spiritual and temporal good | of his native country. | He was uniformly benevolent and courteous | and in private life self-denying and affectionate. | Trusting alone to the merits of Our Lord Jesus Christ | for salvation, he departed this life in the peace of God | on Sunday the 17ᵗʰ Sept. 1871. | "And now, Lord, what wait I for; my hope is in Thee," Psalm xxxix. vii | "We were comforted over you in all our affliction and distress by your faith," I Thess. 3. 7.

Sacred to the memory of | Richard Owen Lloyd Madden | Lieutenant Royal Navy | H.M.S. Osprey | Third son of | John Travers Madden, Eˢᑫ | of Inch House, Co. Dublin. | died at Shanghai, 12ᵗʰ July, 1864. | aged 23 years. | "Behold, He taketh away, who can hinder Him, | who will say unto Him, What doest Thou?" Job. 12. 9.

This tablet was erected by | the Honᵇˡᵉ and Revᵈ Edward Taylor | to the memory of his beloved son | Hercules Langford Barry | who was born June 2ⁿᵈ 1824, | and died January 22ⁿᵈ 1833 : | His soul pleased the Lord, therefore | hasted He to take him to Himself.

Sacred to the Memory | of | The Honorable and Reverend Edward Taylor | youngest son of Thomas, Earl of Bective | Who departed this life at Como in Italy | Loved and lamented | On the 7ᵗʰ of June 1852 | In the 84ᵗʰ year of his age. | "His end was peace." | Also to the memory of | Marianne Harriet, his wife, | Grand-daughter of St. Leger, Viscount Doneraile. | Died 22ⁿᵈ March 1859, aged 78 years.

[NOTE.—The church grounds are not consecrated, as the church stands too close to the town for burials to be sanitary, but there is one grave, that of a former curate who died of cholera. Immediate burial being necessary, he was interred beside the church. The stone is a large flat slab, supported on four large balls of stone, and surrounded by a railing.]—

Underneath | lies interred the mortal remains of | the Rev. Daniel Henry Maunsell | Curate of the Chapel of Balbriggan | who departed this life | on the 15ᵗʰ of July. 1834. | Aged 42 years. | This tomb is erected as a small tribute | to his memory | " So also is the resurrection of the dead.　It is sown in | corruption, it is raised in incorruption ; It is sown in | dishonour, it is raised in glory."　I Cor. 15. 42. 43.

(The only man who had the courage to touch the body of the Rev. W. Maunsell was T. C. G. Hamilton, E^{sq} son of the Rev. George Hamilton of Hampton Hall, Balbriggan.　He coffined the body, and buried it.)

———

' Inscription on a tablet in wall of Balbriggan Harbour ' :—

This pier was built by the | Honble. George Hamilton | of Hampton in the county of Dublin ; | third Baron of His Majesty's Court of Exchequer, | in Ireland ; | whose great object in life was to promote | the trade and prosperity of his country. | Ann. Dom. 1761.

———

## Baldongan Churchyard.

[From Lord Walter FitzGerald.]

' This churchyard is situated about two miles to the north of Lusk on high ground, so that its extensive castle-like ruins can be seen from a long distance.

' The burial-ground occupies the southern side of the ruins, but contains very little of interest.

' The oldest inscribed stone, now visible, is dated as late as 1735.　The inscription is on a rough boulder, and reads ' :—

And^{w} Woott^{on}
died March 29
1735, Aged 27.

———

' The next two inscriptions are copied from headstones ' :—

I.H.S

Here lieth the Body of | Mary O'Neil alias Rogon who | Departed this Life Feb^{y} the 20^{th} | 1784. Aged 32 years Also of her | children.　This Stone Was Erected | by Pat^{k} O'Neil her husband, to | her memory.

———

I.H.S

Here lieth the Body of Margre^{t} | Kelly of Loughshinney who Departed | this Life April y^{e} 27. 1782 Aged 58 yea^{rs} | This Stone was Erected by her husband | Nicholas Rogan to her memory.

## Clondalkin Churchyard.

[From Mr. H. R. Guinness.]

'On a well-preserved tombstone':—

**HEERE VNDER LY-
ETH THE BODY
OF MICHAEL CON-
NOR SHOOMAKE-
R LATE OF DVB-
LIN WHO DEC-
EASED THE 18
DAY OF AVGVST
1643**

## Coolock Churchyard.

[Contributed by Miss A. Peter.]

Here lie the remains of Rhoda, wife of James Wood, Esq$^r$ of Woodville in the County of Sligo, and youngest daughter of Alderman Sir Edmond Nugent of Airfield in this County who departed this life the 8$^{th}$ day of November 1834, Aged 28 years.

Behold he takes away, who can hinder him, who will say unto him what doeth thou Job ? For here have we no continuing city, but we seek one to come.

---

This Stone belongeth to Martin Brownly Rutherford of the City of Dublin, Esq$^r$., & to his Posterity. Underneath are deposited the mortal remains of Jane the affectionate and beloved wife of the said M. B. Rutherford & daughter of Joseph Clarke, M.D., of the city of Dublin. She yielded her Spirit to her God on the 11$^{th}$ day of November 1829, Aged 36 years, full of faith & hope & peace through Christ our Lord, Amen.

---

Beneath this Stone lies interred the body of William Jolly who departed this Life 19$^{th}$ of September 1794, Aged 85 years.

Also of Sarah Jolly his wife, She departed 11$^{th}$ day of December 1799 in the 76$^{th}$ year of her age.

Also the body of Eliza Sophia Jolly, wife of W$^m$ Jolly, Esq$^r$., who departed this Life 23$^{rd}$ of July 1839 Aged 76. Here lieth W$^m$ Jolly son of the two former & husband of M$^{rs}$ Eliza Jolly, who departed 10$^{th}$ of May 1833 Aged 85 years, which long period of his existence he was esteemed a character of good and vertues.

## Cruagh Churchyard.

[From Mr. James R. Fowler.]

'In the centre of the graveyard stands a circular tower of two stories, erected as a look-out for protection against body-snatchers. The upper part could only be reached by a ladder. Steps go down to the lower part, which has an iron-sheathed door. There is a square font lying in the graveyard, cut out of a single granite block, which has an escape hole. Not far from the tower lies a small gable finial, with a top shaped somewhat like a fleur-de-lys.

'Among the inscriptions are':—

Gloria in Excelsis Deo

This Stone was Erected by Rofe Cafey in memory of her Beloved Hufband James Cafey of Temple Oage in the County of Dublin Farmer for him & his Posterity he was a tender Parent and a Faithful Friend much lamented by all who knew him he Departed this life the 21st April in the Year of Our Lord 1800 aged 68 years

Requiescat in Pace

---

+
I H S

This Stone & Burial Place Belongeth to CORNLˢ DONOUGH of Templeoge & his posterity 1760   Here Lyeth the body of ARTHUR DONOUGH Said Cornelius Father Who Departed this Life the 20 day of March 1728 aged 35 years

---

I. H. S.

Here lieth the Body of James Lawless, died May 1760, aged 28 years

---

'There was no trace of the circle-inscribed stone mentioned by Petrie in the Ordnance Survey Correspondence.'

### Drumcondra Churchyard.

[From Miss E. G. O'Mahony.]

' Altar-tomb, N.E. of Vestry ' :—

In the Vault under this Tomb are depoffited [*sic*] the
mortal remains of M<sup>r</sup> Jn° Smart of the City of Dublin
who departed this life in the christian hope
of immortality on the 26<sup>th</sup> day of January 1802
in the 51<sup>st</sup> year of his Age.
He lived beloved and died sincerely regretted
and discharged with tendernefs and integrity
The various relations of Husband Father and Friend.
His affectionate Relict and Childron [*sic*]
have erected this Tomb
to his beloved and lamented Memory
VIRTUTE VIXIT
MEMORIA VIVET
GLORIA VIVET
Also the remains of his grandson Jn° White who
died July 16<sup>th</sup> 1802   Aged 4½ years.

---

' Upright stone N.E. of Vestry ' :—

This Stone belongeth to M<sup>r</sup> | Robert Crotty of Henry
Str<sup>t</sup> | Here Lyeth two of his Sons | Robert and Henry
Sep<sup>r</sup> 3<sup>d</sup> | 1787. |

---

+ ' Upright stone, N.E. part of churchyard, carved with letters
I H S within a circle of rays ; an hour-glass on either side, and
beneath the letters a heart transfixed by two spears.   The piece of
stone bearing the date has scaled off almost completely ' :—

This Stone was erected by M<sup>rs</sup> | Mary Collins of the
Bachelors | Walk Over the Remains of her | Hufband
M<sup>r</sup> Terence Collins who | Departed this Life the 29<sup>th</sup> of
February | 17...   Aged 55 Years |

' Flat tombstone N.E. of Vestry.   Much worn away ' :—

SACRED TO THE MEMORY ⌊OF⌋
MR. PATRICK WHITE
[Who] Departed this Transitory Life on the [23ʳᵈ] of Sepʳ 1794.
[At the] EARLY AGE OF TWENTY SIX years
When Friends and Relatives entertained the moft lively hopes
of the long Enjoyment of his Merits and Virtues.
LEARNED PIOUS BENEVOLENT
FRIENDLY AND AFFECTIONATE
He has left numerous Friends to lament the untimely lofs of
his intrinfic Worth and exemplary Communion.
HEU ! PIETAS ! HEU ! FIDES !

Whoe'er has felt true Friendfhip's facred flame,
Or thinks true Virtue more then empty name,
Oh ! let him this Good Man fincerely mourn,
From faithful friends, from us untimely torn !

* Here lies Also the Body of Elizabeth White
who departed this life on the 31ˢᵗ of December 1855
Aged 100 Years
of your Charity Pray for their Souls.  *
HIS SALTEM ACCUMULEMUS DONIS
ET FUNGIMUR INANI MUNERE !
Requiescant in Pace.   Amen.

[*i.e.*—Let us at least contribute these offerings (the monument,
&c.), and fulfil this useless duty (its erection).]

---

* This part of the inscription has been added by a later hand, some of the
words being engraved over the bearings on the coat-of-arms, making it difficult
to decipher them.   The two Latin lines at the foot of the original epitaph are
so much obliterated that the connecting " up-strokes " of the letters, lightly cut
on the slab, have disappeared.

' S.W. corner, near Lentaigne tomb.   Flat stone, supported (
upright stones ' :—

Gloria in Excelsis

✝
I H S

This Stone was erected by M<sup>rs</sup> C. M<sup>c</sup>Dermott
of the City of Dublin to the Memory
of her beloved Huſband John M<sup>c</sup>Dermott who
departed this life 2<sup>nd</sup> of Auguſt 1799.
Alſo to the memory of Mich<sup>l</sup> & Tho<sup>s</sup> M<sup>c</sup>Dermott
Esq<sup>rs</sup> both Late of the Royal Navy the former
Early fell in the warmth of Youthful daring on
Board his Majesty's Ship the Invincible in the
Memorable Victory Achieved by Rear Admiral
Lord Howe over the French Fleet on the
1<sup>st</sup> June 1794.
The Latter Tho<sup>s</sup> died of a lingering Illneſs on
the 25<sup>th</sup> April 1812   Aged 19 a youth of many
Amible [sic] and excellent qualities.
Requiescant in Pace.

———

' Upright stone, S.W. corner, near sexton's cottage ' :—

This stone was Erected by | Richard Haire in memory
of | his Children James Departed | this Life May 27<sup>th</sup>
1798 Aged | 6 years | Also Mary Dep<sup>d</sup> Decem<sup>r</sup> 23<sup>d</sup>      |
1800 Aged 4 Years |

———

' Upright stone, S.W. corner, close to cottage ' :—

Here lieth the Body of Patrick Bailey | of Marlborough
Street | who departed this life the 5<sup>th</sup> of May | 1800
Aged 50 years | Also his Daughter Elizabeth Harnett |
who Departed this life Feb<sup>y</sup> 20<sup>th</sup> 1804 | Aged 21 Years |
This Stone Erected by her affectionate | Husband
Thomas Harnett as a Just Tribute | to a virtious [sic]
and affectionate Wife. |

———

' Upright stone, S.W., near cottage.   Inscription almoſ
buried ' :—

The Lord gave & the Lord hath | taken away, Bleſsed
be y<sup>e</sup> name | of the Lord. | This Stone & Burial place
belong | to Tho<sup>s</sup> Remminton Late of y<sup>e</sup> | Merchants
Quay, Joyner, who | departed this Life y<sup>e</sup> 7<sup>th</sup> of Decem-
ber | 1761.  Aged [60 ?] years . . . . . . |

' Tablet on north wall of Drumcondra Churchyard, over
ed-in space near the Holy Well of St. John the Baptist ' : —

(Inscription in capital letters throughout.)

Beneath lie the remains of | Anne Johnston | who died
4<sup>th</sup> April 1820, Aet. 11 years. | Also of | Edward Tho<sup>s</sup>
Johnston | who died 28<sup>th</sup> March 1825 Aet. 7 months : |
The beloved children of | Andrew Johnston Esq<sup>r</sup>, M.D. |
[of] Temple S<sup>t</sup> in this city |

---

'' N.E. corner, upright stone, under an ash-tree ' :—

This Stone was erected by Jane Hearn in memory of
her beloved Husband William Hearn late of Bride
Street who departed this Life, on the 14<sup>th</sup> day of Sept.
1807, in the 55<sup>th</sup> Year of his Age.  Here also is interred
the Body of Laurence Hearn Brother of the said
William who died the 12<sup>th</sup> January 1804   Aged 47
Years   Likewise the Body of Johanna Hearn Wife of
James Hearn and Sister-in-law of said William and
Laurence.  She died the 2<sup>nd</sup> day of February 1806
Aged 32 Years.

---

' Upright stone, S.W. corner, near cottage ' :

This Stone Erected to the memory of | Dennis Conran
Died Jan<sup>y</sup> 10<sup>th</sup> A D 1790 |

---

' Fallen stone, N.E. corner, at foot of ash-tree ' :—

Anne White Alias Wentworth | who departed this Life
the 3<sup>rd</sup> of | Octob<sup>r</sup> 1740 in the Fourty Eight | year of
her Age | Here also lieth the Body of Sarah | Shields
Daughter of the above Ann | White and Wife to John
Shields of | the City of Dublin Esq<sup>r</sup> who departed | this
life 11<sup>th</sup> March 1765 Aged 37 years. | Here also lieth
the Body of Elizabeth | Smith Daughter of the above
Ann | White and Wife to James Smith of the | City of
Dublin Esq. who departed this | life 25<sup>th</sup> April 1778
Aged 58 Years. |

---

' Small stone monument, north side of church, shaped like
:ophagus, lying on ground, as if displaced from some larger

pedestal. White marble panels, much discoloured. Inscriptions in small capital letters ' :—

' West Face ' :—

BENEATH THIS STONE ARE
INTERRED THE REMAINS OF
GEORGE LAWRENCE | COYNE NUGENT, ESQ. |
NATUS. JAN. 1810
OBIIT, JUNE, 1829

' Inscription on South face ' :—

Sacred | TO THE MEMORY OF |
JOHN NUGENT ESQ^R
who departed this life April 26^th 1835.
In sure and certain hope of a joyful resurrection
thro CHRIST JESUS.
This Stone is erected by his afflicted Widow
" I shall go to him but he shall not return to me."
2 SAM. XII.

NATUS 14^th July 1808.

' Inscription on East face ' :—

This stone is erected
by her bereaved Mother
to the adored memory of
ALICIA NUGENT
Who died Dec. 19^th 1834
aged 3 years.
Weep not, she is not dead but sleepeth.
LUKE, VIII.

' Inscription on North face ' :—

To the MEMORY of
her BELOVED child
GEORGE NUGENT
who died March 15^th 1835
aged 8 months.
This Stone is erected by his sorrowing mother.
The LORD gave and the LORD hath taken away ;
blessed be the Name of the LORD.
JOB I.

---

## Dublin, Mount Jerome Cemetery.

[From Captain G. S. Cary.]

Sacred to the memory of Captain John Armstrong late of the 12th Royal Veteran Bat^n died 6^th Feb^y 1852 aged 73 years. And his grandson Lindsay P. O'Farrell, Esq^re died 30^th Nov^r 1856 aged 21 [or 24] years. Erected by an affectionate daughter and fond and sorrowing mother.

In Memory of James Stewart, Esq[re] late Captain 87th Royal Irish Fusiliers who departed this life May 20th 1850 aged 68 years. Fanny relict of the late Rev[d] Abraham Augustus Stewart, who died May 12th 1857. Aged 88 years. Also Anna the beloved wife of William Augustus Stewart Esq[re]. late Captain 58th Regiment who departed to be with the Lord June 6th 1864. Aged 63 years. For if we believe that Jesus died and rose again, even so them also which Sleep in Jesus will God bring with Him. 1 Thess IV. 14. W. A. Stewart Esq[re] formerly Captain 58 Reg[t]. Born 4th March 1797. died 23rd Aug[t] 1876.

---

Sacred to the memory of Major Charles Parke, fourth son of Lieut.-Col. Roger Parke of Dunally Co. of Sligo. who departed this life on the 3rd day of November 1858 in his 71st year. This Monument was erected by his nephew Jemmett Duke as a tribute of affection and grateful remembrance.

---

Here lie the remains of the Reverend George Tyrrell of Clonard in the county of Kildare. Obit 5th June 1838.

---

Bryan H. Everard. died April 11th 1838 aged 62 years. J. H. Everard died April 20th 1841. Aged 33 years.

---

Sacred to the memory of Sarah Paton daughter of E. Paton. Arm[r] 42nd R. H. Reg[t]. Wife of Qr Master T[h] Whaite 94th Reg[t]. who died on the 10th of April 1838 in the 20th year of her age, and her infant son.

---

Sacred to the memory of Major Simson Kennedy, late of the 68th Reg[t] who departed this life on the 13th July 1844, aged 72 years. Believe on the Lord Jesus Christ, and thou shalt be saved. Acts 16th Chapter 31st verse.

---

Sacred to the memory of Bridget, Relict of the late Lieut-Colonel W. B. Nicolls, who departed this life on the 11th of June 1845, Aged 67. This stone is placed here by devoted children and marks the spot where rests the remains of their beloved mother. Also to the memory of Deborah Murphy sister of the above who departed this life on the 19th January 1839. Aged 52.

'One side of vault' :—

Sacred to the Memory of Anne Montgomery | Relict of The Late Nathaniel Montgomery of | Dominick S$^t$. And of Swanlinbar in the County of Cavan | Who Departed This Life on The 29th of May 1844 | In the 69th Year of Her Age Her Remains Were | Brought In August 1844 From S$^t$ James church | Yard And Deposited In This Vault |

---

The Remains of Nathaniel Montgomery Esq$^{re}$ | Who Departed This Life | On the 13th of November 1836 Aged 61 Years | And Also Of His Mother-In-Law Geraldine Castle | Who Died The 5th of · December 1822 Aged 85 years | Were Removed from Swanlinbar In the Co. Cavan in | the Month of Sept$^r$ 1844 And Deposited In This Vault. |

---

'NOTE.—Nathaniel Montgomery was born circa 1775, and was the eldest son of Nathaniel Montgomery and Isabella Love, his wife. By his wife, Anne Castle, daughter of John Castle, he had issue Nathaniel Montgomery, who married Amelia Mary Anne, eldest daughter of Colonel Stephen Holmes ; Andrew Castle Montgomery, who married Helen Hill, daughter of Captain Boyle ; Mary, who married John Thompson, of Killabrandish, County Cavan ; and Geraldine, who married John Waring, of Waringfield, County Down.'

---

## Dublin—St. Audoen's Church.

[Contributed by Mr. H. S. Guinness.]

Inscriptions on memorial tablets and tombstones, copied by the late Edward Evans, and published in "The Irish Builder," vol. xxviii, 1886, pp. 320–332.

St. Audoen's Churchyard is now converted into an open space at the west side, on which occasion the tombstones were removed.

---

M. S.

Gulielmi Molyneux Arm ; J. U. D.
In Summâ Cancellariae Hiberniae Curiâ Assessoris ;
Societatis Regiae Londoniensis et Philosophicae Dubliniensis,
Sodalis ;
In Comitiis Parliamentariis Nominae Academiae Patriae
Iterata vice Delegati:
Qui Antiquâ Molyneuxorum stirpe ortus,
Stemmata sua egregiis Meritorum titulis Ornavit.

Familiae eruditae famam
Per Universam Rempublicam literariam Latiùs Sparsit
Abditis Matheseos penetratis
Geometriam, Astronomiam, Dioptricam, Algebramque,
Multis Auxit inventis.
Philosophiae verae ac Utilis incrementa
Studiis et impensis strenuè promovit
Patriae Jura, quae putavit, noto tibi, Viator, Libello
Propugnavit.
Nec moribus minus, quam scientiâ insignis,
Tam supra Piebem vixit, quam sapuit.
Justitiam coluit et pietatem,
Optimorum Amicitiam fide singulari,
Omnium Desiderium Morum suavitate ad se attraxit.
Uti Pater, qui eum genuit, SAMUEL MOLYNEUX Armiger,
Vir, si quis Alius, Moribus Sanctissimis,
Cujus etiam Cinis hic requiescit,
Postquam Annos 77 compleverat.
At filius Proli Dolor ! ex Calculorum in Renibus dolore
Concitato nimis vomitu, venâ disruptâ,
Jugenti Sanguinis Profluvio
Ipso aetatis flore, Anno nempè 42
Animam affudit. Octobris 17, 1698.

NOTE.—A Memoir of William Molyneux is given in "The Irish Builder,"
vol. xxviii, page 320.

———

' On a tombstone in the church ' :—

Here lieth the body of Mr. Thomas Mason, of Chester,
late of the City of Dublin, Merchant, who departed this
life the 25th day of May, 1759. For him and his
Posterity.

Here also lyeth the remains of Mrs. Catherine Townson,
wife of Thos. Townson, of Dolphin's Barn-lane, Tanner,
neice of the above Thos. Mason, who departed this life
the 19th day of November, 1773, aged 42 years.

Also the remains of Mrs. Margaret Johnson, wife of
John Johnson, of Marlborough Street, and Clark of St.
Thomas's, Dublin, niece of the aforesaid Thomas Mason,
and sister of the above Catherine Townson, who departed
this life the 5th day of August, 1779, aged — years.

———

This stone and burial place belong to | Thomas Sheil
and his Posterity. | ·
Here lieth the body of Thomas Sheil | who departed this
life yᵉ 17 June, 1765 aged— |
(The remainder defaced.)

' Another stone records the following ' :—

Here lieth the remains of Mr. Lewis Ward, of Christ Church-yard, in the City of Dublin, who died 6th October 1765, aged 65 years,

Also his wife, Mrs. Mary Ward, who died 28th April, 1787 aged 67.

It may be truly said they were Christians. Most of their grandsons, who died young—Lewis, Benjamin, John, and Joseph Ward—are interred here.

Also the remains of Lewis Denis Ward, son of the above Denis and Mary, late Quarter Master of the III Regt. of Foot, who died in the prime of life, 14th Feb. 1798, aged 44. A brave soldier and a loyal subject.

This stone erected by Mr. Joseph Ward in memory of his dear Parents and a brother ever dear to him.'

---

This stone and burial place belong to Mr. Alex. Gordon, merchant, in Bridge Street.

Here lieth the body of Mrs. Elenor Gordon, wife of said Mr. Gordon, who departed this life the — day of March, 1784, aged 45 years : Also the body of their eldest son, Ellis Gordon, who departed this life, the 22nd Jan. 1797, aged — years : Also the body of their youngest son, W. Gordon, who departed this life the 18th July, 178(4 ?) aged 1 (7 ?) years.

---

Here lies the remains of the late Mr. Joseph Ward, of Bridge Street, merchant, who died 27th May, 1796, aged 68. His daughter Elizabeth died 7th March 1785, aged 19 years.

This tomb was erected by his son in memory of his dear respected father.

---

' The following inscriptions are copied from stones in the graveyard between St. Audoen's Arch and old City Wall ' :—

This stone is sacred to the memory of Sir Anthony King, Knt., Alderman of the City of Dublin, who departed this life 1st Sept. Anno 1787.

His spirited and unwearied exertion as a Magistrate for the Peace and Welfare of the City will ever be remembered with gratitude. The tears of the poor whose necessities he was wont to relieve, bespeak his private virtues.

This stone is also designed to perpetuate the memory

o  Sarah Atkinson, otherwise King, wife of the above
Sir Anth^y King.
Here lyes also the body of Anthony King, Esq., Son of
the above-named Sir Anthony King, who dyed the 19^th
day of September Anno 1797.  Aged 55 years.

---

Simulator nunquam et probitatis et charitatis pro virili
cultor expectavit dum fuit in mundo exitium quod vita
etiam innoccua ne quis conciliare possit spe caelestium
spretis terrenis quiescit tandem in pace.
And beneath this stone rest the remains of Mrs. Jane
King, wife of Anthony King, Esq., who died anno 1812,
Aged 60.  Also much esteemed and regretted.
Filius ejus natu maximus tutoram maerens posuit.

---

Erected in memory of John Birkett, of Whitehaven,
Mariner, who departed this life the 18th August 1788,
Aged 64.

---

This stone was erected to the memory of William
Doolittle, of Bridge Street, in the city of Dublin,
merchant, and his sister, Elizabeth Doolittle, otherwise
Slator, who departed this life the 14th of August, 1796,
both aged 48 years.  Who, whilst they lived, loved and
feared God, and was affectionate and kind to each other,
wel(l) loved and respected by all their acquaintance,
(and) happy are they who are in such a state (pre)pared
at all times to meet their God.  (Here also) lieth 4 of
their children.

---

Here lieth the body of Mr. Andrew Wildsam, Who died
1Cth Feb^y. 1804.  Aged 75 years  Also Mrs Sarah
Wildsam his wife (Who) died 20th June (1814)  Aged
(58 ?) years.

---

This stone was erected by Mr. James King, Manufac-
turer in Glasgow, in memory of his brother, Mr. John
King formerly of the Parish of Kilmadock, in the Co.
of Perth, Scotland, but late of King's Inns Quay, City
of Dublin.  He departed this life the 1 (?) of May, 1804
aged 5(0) years

Erected by Marg$^t$. Ellen Boyde to the memory of her beloved Husband, John Boyde, who departed this life on the 10th day of January, 1836, aged 36 years. Also their only and beloved child John William Boyde, who died the 26th April, 1837, aged two years and ten months.

---

This stone and burial place belong to Terence Newland and his posterity  .   .   .   .   .   ,

---

Erected by Nicholas Mahon, of the Merchant's Quay in the city of Dublin, Merchant, in memory of his wife, Mrs Margaret Mahon, who lies here interred, and departed this life on the 20th May, 1811, in the 44 year of her age, Beloved and lamented by her Family and numerous friends. Here also lies interred their son Mort. Mahon who died at the age of 3 years. And his second beloved son Nicholas Mahon, who died on the 14th day of March, 1822, aged 14 years. Likewise his elder Brother, James Mahon, Esq., of Limerick, who departed this life on the 5th April 1832, aged 93 years. And herein lies the remains of the above named Nicholas Mahon, who departed this life on the 5th day of May, 1841, aged 95 years, who was an eminent merchant in this Parish for upwards of 70 years. And herein also lie the remains of his sisters-in-law Miss Bridget and Elenor Mahon  Requiescant in Pace. Amen.

---

Here lies the body of George Hill, Esq. He was removed from this mortal scene on the 24th of January, 1812, at the age of 54 years. Here also lie the remains of his beloved wife Mary Hill Who was removed to her rest on the 15th of December, 1843 At the age of 79 years. Likewise George Henry Brown Aged 5 years Died 6th July, 1333

---

Erected by Peter and Frances Hallion, in memory of their beloved son George Peter Hallion who departed this life April 23rd, 1822  Aged 13 years  Also Ann, sister to the above who departed this life April 20th, 1828, aged 35 years. Here also lie the remains of the said Peter Hallion Father of the above children, who departed this life on the 7th day of January, 1837, aged 74 years. Also the remains of the said Frances Hallion, Mother of the above children, who departed this life on the 14th May, 1851, aged 84 years.

'On the wall filling up one of the ornamental arches on south ide (inside) of church are two marble tablets, on one of which is he following inscription ' :—

> Sacred to the memory of Thomas Evory Esq. M.D., late of the city of Dublin. He was born in Londonderry on the 18th of October in the year 1758, and died at his house in Rutland Square, January 10th 1828 Eminent in his profession and deservedly esteemed he will long be extensively regretted This monument is erected by his affectionate sister.

----

'On the second of the pair of tablets already mentioned is the ollowing inscription ' :—

> " Sacred to the memory of Margaret Evory, of the city of Dublin, Spinster. She survived her brother, the late Thomas Evory, Esq. M.D., three years and departed this life at her own house on the 12th of February, 1831, aged 76 years. This monument was erected by her residuary Legatees "

----

> To the memory of Mrs. Margaret O'Neill, relict of John O'Neill Esq., of Kells, Co. Meath. She departed this life 23rd June, 1831, aged 60 years. And to her grandson, Henry Kamptee Keating, A.B., T.C.D., Surgeon, son of Capt. Henry Keating, of Millsbrook, Oldcastle; and of the Madras Army. He departed this life 26th of March, 1849, aged 23 years. Also to the above named Captain Henry Keating Who died 15th October, 1851, aged 60 years.

----

'Inside church, in south aisle, east end' :—

> Here lieth the body of Lieutenant Roger Coghlan, 83rd Regiment, who died the 28th March, 1834 Aged 24 years.

----

'In the eastern half of north side chancel' :—

> Sacred to the memory of Colonel John Staunton Rochfort, of Clogrenane, Co. Carlow, Whose mortal remains lie interred in the adjoining grave, He departed this life on the 5th May, 1844, Aged 81 years.

Sacred to the memory of Sarah Deborah Rochfort, the beloved wife of the Rev. Henry Rochfort, Rector of Castletown, Who departed this life the 28th June, 1837, Aged 40 years. Also sacred to the memory of Mary Alice, who died January 18th, 1837, aged nine months And Mervyn Archdall, who died May 25th, 1837, Aged 15 years. The infant children of the Rev Henry Rochfort and Sarah Deborah his wife.

---

Erected by Edward Constable as a mark of affection to his beloved mother Mrs Anne Constable, who departed this life the 4th of February, 1852, aged 60 years.

---

Underneath this is laid the remains of Mr. William Somerville, 2nd brother of Sir Quaile Somerville. Bart. Also the remains of his wife Mrs. Elizabeth Somerville aged 61, who departed this life March the 11th, 1817. To an exterior, peculiarly engaging, she united a good mind and simplicity of heart rarely to be met with, respected and beloved. May those who mourn her emulate her in her many virtues.

---

## Dublin, St. Kevin's Old Churchyard.

[From the Rev. R. S. Maffett, b.a.]

(*Continued from p.* 321, *Vol. VII.*)

' Row IV, No. 1.—The surface of this headstone has all flaked off ; and if there was ever any lettering on it, it is now completely gone.'

---

' No. 2.—A headstone, about a foot from the last, stands at the south of No. 1 of Row III. There was possibly nothing more ever inscribed on this memorial than the I H S, with cross above, and the carving contained in brackets, which is to the left hand of the centre of the I H S. What has been given as " 8 " looks, however, more like " S " ':—

I.H.S.

[? 1810]

' No. 3.—This headstone, which is in front of No. 2 of Row III, has, under the I H S, with cross above, a device resembling a broad arrow. If there is anything more on the stone, it must be after a greater space than that between the lines recorded ' :—

This Stone & Burial Place | belong to Mr, Charles | Doyle of Fleet Street, | Grocer, & his Pofterity, | Here lieth the Body of M$^{rs}$ | Anne Doyle, Wife of faid | Charles Doyle, who departed | this Life the 6$^{th}$ of April, 1774 | in the 70$^{th}$ Year of her Age | Also the Body of the said | Charles Doyle, who departed | This Life the 3$^{d}$ of June, 1775, | Jn (*sic*) the 77$^{th}$ year of his age

---

' No. 4 is a slate headstone a little behind the line of No. 3, and some four feet to the north of it ' :—

SACRED
To the Memory of
MRS. MARY NOLAN ELRINGTON,
The lamented and honored Wife of
STEPHEN NOLAN ELRINGTON, OF LIMERICK CITY,
Obiit 12th May 1833,
Aged 42 Years.

Thy fireside was thy world, its homely hearth
Was dearer than the palace of the proud ;
Thy Children gath'ring round its blaze in mirth,
Could give more pleasure than the worthless crowd.
The pride of life—its pomp—its vanity,
In thee found not a heart that could approve,
For thine was full of pure humility,
Calm resignation and domestic love.

Here also " sleep in Jesus," their Children, | Martin N. Elrington, an Infant, Obiit 9$^{th}$ June 1826. | James N. Elrington, Obiit 20$^{th}$ April 1828. | Frances Maria N. Elrington, Obiit 28$^{th}$ August 1834.

---

' No. 5 is a large flat stone close to the last, but with its head some three feet behind the line of No. 4. According to the Post

Office Directory for 1832 Mr. William Furlong, 22 Upper Fitz-william Street, and 60 Aungier Street, was an attorney (? Furlong and La Touche, attornies, 60 Aungier Street) ' :—

> Here lieth the Remains of | the undernamed Children of | WILLIAM & SARAH FURLONG | of Fitzwilliam Street. | WILLIAM EDWARD died 11ᵗʰ Septʳ 1821. | JOHN GEORGE 13ᵗʰ | WILLIAM CROKER 1ˢᵗ Janʸ 1825. | JOHN 28ᵗʰ July 1830. | SARAH MARIA 23ʳᵈ March 1833 : | *all under the age of One year.*

---

' No. 6.—Less than a foot from the last memorial is a flat lime-stone slab four feet long by three and a half feet wide, resting on four granite steps or bases. The highest of these does not project at the foot of the slab, and to a small extent only at the head, but about six inches at each side. The lowest is very much disarranged and measures from twenty-one to twenty-eight inches in projection from that resting on it, and each of the second and third bases from eleven to fourteen inches. These steps are covered with long grass, and altogether are in a discreditable state, and require the attention of the deceased's relatives, if any such are alive. I believe the year of Mr. O'Connor's death to be correctly given below as carved on the stone, though his name does not disappear, as minister of St. Luke's, from " Wilson's Dublin Directory " till 1824. According to " Erck's Ecclesiastical Register " for 1818, he was appointed to St. Luke's in 1810, and if he belonged to Trinity College, Dublin, his M.A. degree is not recorded in " Todd's Cata-logue," 1869, but only his B.A., which he would seem to have taken in 1783 ' :—

> Sacred | to the Memory of | The Revᵈ WILLIAM O'CONNOR. A.M. | Minister of the Parish of Sᵗ Luke in this Diocess : | whose real but unostentatious Charity, | Sincerity of heart, | faithful discharge of the duties of his function, | and many social virtues, of a tender Husband, | affectionate Father, and a steady friend : | endear'd him to all who knew him in life, | and deplore him in death. | He departed this life on the 8ᵗʰ of March 18[22] | Aged 6[?2] years. | His disconsolate widow has erected this | Monument, to mark the spot that | contains his beloved remains, together | with those of his Mother, and six of | his Children who died in Infancy.

---

' No. 7.—A flat stone originally about a foot probably from the last memorial ; though a letter or two of the inscription, especially he " H " in brackets, is now concealed by the disarranged step or base of No. 6. There is a curved stroke, apparently carved, under the last two figures of the first year ':—

> Here Lyeth the Body of William Lane of the | City of Dublin Esq$^r$ who Departed this Life, | The 23$^{rd}$ day of January 1778, in the 66$^{th}$ Year | of his age. | He Lived Esteemed and died Regretted by all | His Acquaintance | [H]ERE ALSO LIETH THE REMAINS OF HIS COUSIN | JAMES BIGGER | WHO DEPARTED THIS LIFE 19$^{TH}$ OF JANUARY 1868 | AGED 54 YEARS. | LIKEWISE HIS WIFE | JANE BIGGER | WHO DEPARTED THIS LIFE 8$^{TH}$ OF JANUARY 1867 | AT AN ADVANCED AGE.

---

' No. 8 is an altar-tomb with granite sides and ends and a limestone slab on the top. It is close to the last memorial and bears the following inscription ' :—

> Here lieth the Body of Iames Ennis late of
> Stillorgan in the County of Dublin Gent who
> Departed this Life the [6$^{th}$ ?] Day of Iuly 1780
> Aged 60 years.
> This Stone was Erected by his Widow Ann Ennis
> [a]s a Mark of her Love and affection for him

> Here lieth the Body of M$^{rs}$ Ann Waldron
> Wife of Henry Waldron of Stillorgan Esq$^r$
> who departed this Life the 3$^{rd}$ of Aug$^t$ 1790
> Aged 50 years.
> In her was [sic] centred all the Qualities that
> form the tender Wife the sincere Friend
> and the benevolent Christian

---

' No. 9 is a headstone of limestone about a foot and a half from the last, sunk in the ground and leaning forward. There is nothing more on this stone except it be much further down. The figure in brackets might possibly be " 8 " ' :—

> Here Lieth the Body of | Thomas Woolridge, who departed this | life the 28$^{th}$ of Nov$^r$ 1802 aged 48 Years | Also the Body of his Daughter, M$^{rs}$ | Maria Forbes of Artane County of | Dublin, departed this Life 3$^{rd}$ March 1809 | aged 2(3) years.

---

' No. 10 is a tall headstone of limestone on a granite base. It is on a line with No. 8, close to but somewhat behind the last memorial. At the beginning of the eighth line there is a space hollowed out, where no doubt some wrong lettering was at first carved. The verses sadly contrast with the present gloomy appearance of this churchyard, there being, as far as I am aware, no flowers in it now ' :—

> Sacred | to the memory of M<sup>r</sup> JOHN BROWNE Late | of Bray who departed this life 11<sup>th</sup> Janr<sup>y</sup> | 1817 Aged 52 Years. | Also his beloved wife LETITIA died 29<sup>th</sup> | April 1834 Aged 73 Years. | Their Grandaughter [sic] LETITIA ANNE | died June 4<sup>th</sup> 1834 | Aged 2 Years & three months. | This Stone was Erected by their Sons W<sup>m</sup> | & TH0<sup>s</sup> BROWNE as a mark of gratitude | to the memory of their beloved Parents.

> YET SHALL THY GRAVE WITH RISING FLOWERS BE DRESE'D, [sic]
> AND THE GREEN TURF LIE LIGHTLY ON THY BREASTS, [sic]
> HERE SHALL THE MORN HER EARLIEST TEARS BESTOW,
> HERE THE FIRST ROSES OF THE YEAR SHALL BLOW,
> WHILE ANGELS WITH THEIR SILVER WINGS O'ERSHADE,
> THE GROUND NOW SACRED BY THY DEAR MEMORYS BED.

> Also to the memory of | Esther the Beloved Wife of | the above named WILLIAM BROWNE | who departed this life April 28<sup>th</sup> 1857 | SHE | " IS NOT LOST BUT GONE BEFORE." | Also to the memory of the above named | WILLIAM BROWNE who departed this life | January 14<sup>th</sup> 1860 Aged 69 years. | Also to the memory of the above named | THOMAS BROWNE who departed this life | October 14<sup>th</sup> 1861 Aged 63 Years.

---

' No. 11 is a flat stone about half a foot from No. 10. Apparently there was never any inscription on it.'

---

' No. 12 is a headstone of limestone half a foot from the last, and leaning a little forward. The first letter of " Liskennet " is an E without the head horizontal line, but the place is probably a townland in Ballingarry parish ' :—

> This Stone is Erected to the memory | of John Somers, formerly of Liskennet | County of Limerick & late of Camden | Street Dublin, who departed this life | April 20 1817, Aged 65 Years.

---

' No. 13 is a small upright stone with rounded head, and only one foot in width. It stands some three and a half feet from No. 12, and almost as much to the east of the line of that memorial. The date of death was covered with earth, only about seven

inches of the stone being above ground.   It is not likely that there is
any further inscription.   The lettering is altogether in capitals ' —:

> HEAR (*sic*) LYE [TH ?]
> Y<sup>E</sup> BODY OF [M ?]
> RICHA<sup>RD</sup> COE[Y]
> WHO DEPART [E ?]
> Y<sup>S</sup> LIFE Y<sup>[E ?]</sup> 26<sup>[TH?]</sup>
> OF AVG<sup>ST</sup> 1712
> & Y<sup>E</sup> 60<sup>TH</sup> YEARE [*sic*]
> OF HIS AGE

---

' No. 14.—A headstone of limestone, sunk to the south and
leaning back a little.   It is some five and a half feet from the
last ' :—

> Here lyeth Interred the Remains | of M<sup>rs</sup> Jane Young
> who departed | this Life 5<sup>th</sup> July 1789 Aged 84 Years |
> Beloved and Respected by all | her Acquaintance.

---

' No. 15.—Some four feet from the previous memorial is a limestone slab resting on four freestone supports, one of which at least
will soon have crumbled away altogether.   These were probably
the supports of the original stone, on which they were placed when
it was laid on the ground, and the later slab erected.   The head of
the tomb is about two feet to the west of the line of No. 14.   The
" c " and " t " are connected with each other at the top in the
word " acted," and in " Thomb " there is a horizontal stroke
carved by mistake at the top of the " h," like that of another
capital " T " ' :—

> The moft Reverend Father in God
> William King
> Lord arch Bishop [*sic*] of Dublin
> Caused this Monument to be Erected
> as a Testimony
> of the respect he had
> for
> Henry Greene
> Who was Born on the 1<sup>st</sup> day of March 1668
> and died on the 16<sup>th</sup> day of June 1715
> and who Acted
> Upwards of 20 Years
> as Receiver of his Graces Rents.
> Here alfo lie the Bodies of W- Greene Nephew
> to the Before Named Henry Greene
> and of Catherine his Wife

also
The Bodies of Several of the
Children and Grandchildren of the Said
W<sup>m</sup> and Catherine Greene
by whose descendants
this Thomb [*sic*] was Repaired on the
Eleventh day of March
A.D. 1796.
Also the remains of Elizabeth Greene
died 4<sup>th</sup> March 1857, Aged 15 years.
with her Mother Maria Greene
died 11<sup>th</sup> March 1862, Aged 47 years.

———

The inscription on the old slab and those on the few remaining stones in this row I hope to contribute next time.

———

'The following inscription is taken from a low altar-tomb at the extreme east of the churchyard, not very far from the north boundary. The limestone slab bearing it has, at the top, the third and last coat-of-arms which I have found in this ground, a rubbing of which I have taken to accompany this note. The sides of the tomb and the kerbing are of granite, the north and east portions of the latter being covered up. Remains of railings are in the kerb at the west end, and such also appear above ground at the east. These latter stand about two feet from the middle house of three, which form part of the east boundary—the northernmost one being that allotted to the sexton to live in. The frontage of these houses is in Liberty Lane, off Camden Row. The inscription is in small letters. The last letter in " stric(test ?) " is a perpendicular stroke too tall for that of a " t "; it resembles an " f," but there does not seem room for " of." I am not aware whether there was any relationship between this Thomas Greene and the " Henry Greene " of Row iv, No. 15. A " Pedigree of the Greene Family " was published by the late Surgeon-Colonel Greene, the few remaining copies of which were lately offered for sale at Greene's Library, Clare Street, but I have not seen this volume.

'The crest appears to be a stag's head; and the arms, " azure, three stags trippant." The motto is : " I neither fear nor despise ' " :—

Sacred to the Memory
of
Thomas Greene
Eminently diftinguifhed
For all the Social Virtues
He was a loyal Subject

**THE GREENE FAMILY ARMS ON A TOMB IN ST. KEVIN'S OLD CHURCHYARD, DUBLIN.**

[*From a rubbing by the Rev. R. S. Maffett.*]

A Patriot Citizen
Faithful in Truſt
In Friendſhip candid and Sincere
Univerſally beloved in Life
And not leſs Lamented in Death
Having lived up to the Stric [teft ?] Rules
of Morality an[d] [R]eligion
He Exchanged this Life for a better
On the fifth day of Iune 1760
In the 54ᵗʰ year of his Age
This Monument was erected
by his Widow
In the year of our Lord MDC[CLX]IV

---

[CORPORATION OF FELTMAKERS.]

' Some 7 or 8 feet to the south of the side wall of the church, at its centre, is to be found an interesting altar-tomb bearing the oldest date in the churchyard, as far as I have yet ascertained. The brickwork of which the underpart is composed is broken away at the foot. This memorial is not so high as the " Leeson " tomb, a few feet to the south-west of which it stands, and which the old sexton had thought to have the oldest date in the graveyard when I copied the inscription carved on it (see vol. vi, p. 287). When looking through the churchyard, however, along with the caretaker, one evening in the autumn of 1909 I observed "1706" on this stone, and then carefully examined the inscription for an older date, which I found. The upper part of the slab, however, was so concealed by a layer of a greasy, greenish substance that I had to get it cleaned by more than one application of hot water, in which " washing soda " was dissolved.

' With respect to the inscriptions, which are in capitals, " Damaske Street " is Dame Street ; the " Y's " are of the form of our small " ʸ," but do not descend below the other lettering, and the last two letters of the fifth line are conjoined ; the upper part of the 8 resembles an inverted triangle. The second inscription runs continuously with the first as regards the space between the lines : it is, however, evidently more recently cut and only the larger capitals are of the same size as the older lettering. The " U's " of the later inscription are of the form of our small " u," unlike those of the older, which are " V's.' The last lines give the names of the " Master " and two " Wardens " of the year. After copying the inscription I began to take (a matter of considerable difficulty) a rubbing of the stone, which I hope to finish and send with my next notes.

' The existing registers of St. Peter's Parish do not begin at so early a date as 1668. See the JOURNAL of the R.S.A.I. for December, 1905, for a note on this Corporation of Feltmakers, the belongings of which have, I believe, been recovered since then ' :—

> HERE · LIETH · INTERRED
> THE · BODY · OF · NATHANIELL [*sic*]
> CARTWRIGHT · FELTMAKER · IN
> DVBLIN · OF · DAMASKE · STREETE
> WHO · DEPARTED · THIS · LIFE · THE
> 15 · DAY · OF · IVLY · AN[NO · D]OMI
> NI · 1668 · H[ER]E · L[IET]H · A[LS]O
> THE · BODIES · OF · EIGHT · OF · HIS
> CHILDREN · BETWIXT · HIM
> AND · THE · CHVRCH
> THIS TOMB WAS REBUILT AT
> THE CHARGE OF THE CORPOR
> ATION OF FELTMAKERS OF DUB
> LIN 1706 RICHARD FAULKNER
> MASTER IOHN DITCHFIELD
> WALTER BEVIN WARDENS

## Dublin, St. Luke's Church.

[From Mrs. T. Long.]

Sacred to the memory of the | Rev^d Arthur Burroughs | formerly Minister of this Parish who while in the pride of life | and in the midst of the most active and | faithful exercise of ministerial duties | was by the decree of an all wise GOD | suddenly called away. | His sorrowing congregation | so often edified by his instruction comforted by | his sympathy and animated by his example, | have erected this votive tablet earnestly desiring | that they may be followers of him as he was of | Christ Jesus. | Died 13^th April 1836 aged 37 years. |

In memory of | Walter Thom Esq. | Author of the " History of Aberdeen &c &c " | died 16th of June 1824 aged 54 years. | and | Margaret Turner his wife | died 4^th May 1842 aged 73 years | both interred in the adjoining churchyard. | This tablet has been erected by his son | Alex^r Thom Abbey St. Dublin. |

'Pulpit. (A brass.')

To the | glory of GOD | and in memory of the noble Huguenots | who came to this Parish | from their native France | for liberty of conscience | this pulpit was erected by | Mrs C. E. Smylie St Luke's Rectory | S^{th} Cir^r Road Christmas 1899.

———

This burial place belong | eth to M^r John Banks first | Sexton of St. Luke's and his | posterity. Qui obiit Aug. 26 | 1732 ætatis suæ 70. | (Another short line illegible.)

———

This stone & burial | place belongeth to M^r William | Dally Cloathier and his posterity. | Here lieth the body of the above | William Dally | who departed this life the 12^{th} | day of June 1735 | Aged 48 years. | Here also lyeth 6 of his children. |

———

This stone and Burial | Place belongeth | to the Family of M^r Walter Decauan (?)  .  .  .  .   27 1720   Aged 67 years. |  .  .  .  .  Dorothy Walker—wife of M^r Thomas Robert Decauan 1727  .  .  .  .  .  .  .

———

This stone | is erected by Sarah Bryan | of Brabazon Street in memory | of her father and mother William | and Sarah Pennell who are both | interred here and also their three sons, | viz. William, Thomas and John Pennell late of Brabazon | St Anno Domini 1788.

———

Here lieth the body | of M^r William Fisher | of Hanover St who | departed this life the 10^{th} of | Dec. 1796.

———

Eheu fugit irreparabile tempus.

Beneath lie the remains of James | Wallace who departed this life | Feb | 15^{th}, Anno Dom. 1792 and also those | of Deborah his wife qui obiit Jan. 3^{rd}. | Anno 1792

This stone was erected by | Isabella Browne in memory
of | her husband John Browne | who departed this life
November | the 18<sup>th</sup> 1799 aged 84 years. | Here also
lieth the remains of his | mother and 6 of his children. |
Underneath dothe lie | as much virtue as could die |
The orphan's friend | The widow's sure repose | and
child of sorrows . . . . | When he knew their
woes. |

---

Francis Hussey | Tanner, 1719. (Stone in church wall.)

---

Here lieth the remains of M<sup>r</sup> John Flanagan | of
Summer Hill Dublin. | A Man of singular benevolence
of mind | and goodness of heart | an affectionate hus-
band and | firm friend. | He merited the esteem of all,
the enmity of none. | His affectionate widow erected
this stone | in testimony of her love for him while
living | and to perpetuate his memory as now dead. |
He died on the 20<sup>th</sup> July, 1796 | in the 44<sup>th</sup> year of his
age. |

---

This stone was erected by Mr Charles Haskins | of
. . . . Street for him and his posterity. | Here
lieth the bodies of 5 of his children. | Arthur Haskins
died Nov. 29<sup>th</sup> 1791. | aged 14 months. | Richard who
died July 1792 aged 4 months. | Elizabeth who died
June 29<sup>th</sup> 1796 | aged     months | Charles who died
April 1799 aged 3 years | William who died Jan 12.
1801. aged 7 years. |

---

Here lieth the body of Joseph M<sup>c</sup>Nab, of the City of
Dublin | who departed this life | the 8th of April 1778
aged 36. | Also the body of Marebell his wife | who
departed this life | 19<sup>th</sup> May 1772 | aged 48 | and the
body of Theophilus their | son who died 16<sup>th</sup> of May.
1773. aged 26. and 8 of their children | Here lieth the
body of Ann | McNab who died 20<sup>th</sup> June 1781.

---

Eliz<sup>th</sup>. Lewis has | this stone erected to the | memory
of her dearly beloved | and affectionate husband | W<sup>m</sup>
Lewis who departed this | life in hope of a joyful
resurrection | the 18<sup>th</sup> of October 1782 | Here lieth their
well | beloved | and darling son Solomon Lewis | who

died the 7<sup>th</sup> of May 1782 aged 4 years | and six months and four of their | children who died young. | Here lieth the body of the | above Eliz<sup>th</sup> Lewis who departed | this life Jan' | 19<sup>th</sup> 1792 aged 49 years. |

---

Here lieth the body of the Hon<sup>ble</sup>. Robert Hellen | Second Justice of His Majesty's Court of Common Pleas | who departed this life the 22<sup>nd</sup> day of July 1793 | aged 65 years. | Here also lies the body of Robert Hellen | son to the late Judge Hellen | who died on the first of March 1796 | aged 39 years. | Here also lies the remains of Mrs. Dorothea Hellen | his wife who departed this life 23<sup>rd</sup> June 1806 aged 78 years. |

---

Here lieth the body of, | M<sup>rs</sup> Barbara Parker | who departed this life March 21<sup>st</sup>. 1807 | aged 41 years. | Here also lieth the body of her husband | John Parker Esq<sup>re</sup> of G<sup>t</sup> Britain St | who departed this life August the 20<sup>th</sup> 1832 | aged 85 years. | This stone was erected by their surviving children | as a memorial of their love and affection. | Also Catherine Haslam their daughter | on the 19<sup>th</sup> of March 1840 aged 36 years. | Elizabeth Parker died April 1870 | aged 79 years | Thomas Parker September 24<sup>th</sup> 1883 aged 84 years | Alice Parker died March 29<sup>th</sup> 1892 | aged 80. |

---

Sacred to the memory of Mr Sam<sup>l</sup> Davis | who died 1819 aged 85. | Also of his widow | M<sup>rs</sup>. Elizabeth Davis | who died Jan 1825 | aged 70. | Here also are | interred his son | M<sup>r</sup> John Davis | who died Dec 1815 aged 31. | and also his grandson, | John Davis | who died 2<sup>nd</sup> August 1825. | aged 17. | also Francis Davis his grandson | who died on the 13<sup>th</sup> of April, 1877 aged 45 years. |

---

Here lieth the body of | Mark Sanders | Brabazon Row who departed this life the 1<sup>st</sup> day of May 1831 (?) | in the 75<sup>th</sup> year of his age. | (Some more lines illegible.)

---

Here lieth the body of Rebecca Ross | who departed this life 28<sup>th</sup> March 1812 | aged 69 years. | Also the body of her husband | Alexander Ross Esq<sup>re</sup> | who departed this life Sept<sup>r</sup>. 26<sup>th</sup> 1835 | aged 71 years. |

Underneath are deposited the remains | of Mr William Bernard late of Usher's Quay | who departed this life 5<sup>th</sup> March 1812 | aged 33 years. | This stone has been placed here by his | affectionate widow M<sup>rs</sup> Rachael Bernard as | a small but sincere token of her affection | and respect for his memory. Here also rest the remains of | Mr Michael Browne Grand father of | the above M<sup>rs</sup> Bernard | to whose posterity the burial ground belongs. |

---

Erected by M<sup>r</sup> Edward Clarke of Cork St | in memory of his brother M<sup>r</sup> Rich<sup>d</sup> Clarke | late of New Market Coombe. | Also his brothers wife Mary Jane Clarke | who departed this life 8<sup>th</sup> of Dec<sup>r</sup>, 1829 | aged 60 years. | Rich<sup>d</sup> Clarke departed this life | 30<sup>th</sup> of Jan<sup>y</sup> 1834 aged 71 years. | Here also are interred the remains | of the above M<sup>r</sup> Edward Clarke who | departed this life March 1846 | aged 78 years. |

---

Sacred to the memory of | M<sup>rs</sup> Rachel Wallnutt | late of Kingstown in the County of Dublin | who departed this life the 14<sup>th</sup> of August 1830 | aged 75 years. | Also her husband | John Wallnutt Esq<sup>re</sup> | who departed this life the 26<sup>th</sup> of Oct<sup>r</sup> 1832 | aged 82 years | Fifty years of which he held a commission in his Majesty's service. | Beloved by all who knew him | An humble Christian, | a tender husband | an affectionate father | and faithful friend | Beloved in life and in death lamented. | Erected by their affectionate daughter | Anne Kirwan | as a token of gratitude to her beloved Parents, | IV Chap. XIII verse, I Thess.,—I would not have you to be ignorant | brethren, concerning them which are asleep, that ye sorrow not even as others which have no hope. Also three of her children who died young.

---

This stone and burial ground | belongeth to | M<sup>r</sup> W<sup>m</sup> Richey of Hanover Street, silk manufacturer | Underneath are deposited the remains of | his beloved wife Anne | aged 29 years. | Also his son Samuel aged 4 years. | and John, 23 years | his daughter Esther 2 years | and other children who died young. | Here are interred the mortal | remains of M<sup>rs</sup> Mary Sherwood | daughter of the above W<sup>m</sup> and Anne | who departed this life the 14<sup>th</sup> of June 1839 | aged 39 years. | also his father M$^r$ Samuel Richey of | the Coombe aged 84 years and his mother, | M$^{rs}$ Mary Richey aged 60 | years His 2 sisters M$^{rs}$ Mary Toucher aged 36 | years and M$^{rs}$ Alice Delany aged 40 years. | His brother M$^r$ John Richey departed | this life May 10$^{th}$ 1830 aged 79 years. | Mrs M, A, Richey wife of said Mr W$^m$ Richey | Ob$^t$ 9$^{th}$ Dec$^r$ 1848 aged 77. | Also William Frederick Richey Esq$^{re}$ M.D. | son of the above William and Mary Anne Richey | who departed this life 26$^{th}$ Jan$^y$, 1851 aged 38 years. |

---

‘ The Atkinson monument. At the head of this stone lies a very old one, which the sexton says is an earlier Atkinson stone, and that the date of it is 1711. Only a letter here and there on it can be made out. 171 is plain ’ :—

This stone is erected by M$^{rs}$ Eleanor Atkinson | of Spitalfields | Dublin | in memory of her | Deceased husband M$^r$ Richard Atkinson who | departed this life 22$^{nd}$ of September | 1790 aged 53 years | Here also are deposited the bodies of the | undernamed children. | John, Elizabeth, Mary, William, Thomas, Eleanor | also here lieth the body of M$^r$ Rich$^d$ Atkinson | who departed this life the 24$^{th}$ day of October 1813 | aged 45 years. | Here also lieth the body of M$^{rs}$ Sarah Mullen | who departed this life 26$^{th}$ February 1814 | aged 51 years | She was an affectionate Parent and loving wife | and a sincere friend who lived much esteemed and died much regretted by all her friends . . | W$^m$ Atkinson died July 1802 aged 31. | Mary wife of Tho$^s$ died 19$^{th}$ July 1819 | Robert died 28$^{th}$ April 1826 aged 46. | Thomas died 27$^{th}$ of March 1828 aged 49. | Elizabeth Relict of William Atkinson died Jan$^y$ 1837 aged 65 years. | Caroline A. the beloved wife of Rich$^d$ Atkinson | of College Green Dublin died 22$^{nd}$ May 1827 aged 33. | A century having elapsed since this stone was erected | it was put in a perfect state of repair the year of our LORD 1857 | by the Right Hon$^{ble}$ Richard Atkinson | Lord Mayor of the City of Dublin | son of William Atkinson Woollen manufacturer Pimlico | who departed this life in 1802 and grandson of | Mrs Eleanor Atkinson who erected this tombstone | and who died 19$^{th}$ Sept$^r$ 1819 aged 76 | Richard Charles only son of the above Richard and Caroline Atkinson | died 27$^{th}$ of May 1859 | Also Richard Atkinson a second time Lord Mayor of Dublin | died 19$^{th}$ July 1866 aged 70 years. |

## Dublin, St. Mary's Church, Mary Street.

[From Mrs. T. Long.]

'Inscriptions from monuments inside the church' :—

To the memory | of | the Right Reverend Father | in GOD | Edward Tenison. D.D. | Late Lord Bishop of Ossory | who departed this life November 29th A.D. 1735 in the 62nd year of his age. Anne Tenison | his beloved wife | caused this monument to be erected.

---

Near this place | lieth the Body of M[rs] Chenevix | Daughter of the late Colonel Dives of Bedfordshire | and wife to the Right Reverend Richard | Lord Bishop of Waterford and Lismore. A lady formed by Divine Providence | for the Residence of all Christian virtue & every amiable quality. To her superior understanding | Improved by a generous education & much reading| were joined a benevolent & obliging disposition | and an affable and courteous Deportment. Which with a peculiar liveliness of spirit | rendered her conversation entertaining and instructive. and qualified her to sustain the different stations of life | in which she appeared, with high reputation | she abounded with the truest signs of a most affectionate tenderness towards her husband and of kindness to her relatives. and of charity to the poor. In return for these excellencies she was loved & esteemed by all that knew her. | particularly by her Royal Mistress the Princess | of Orange & her friend the Countess of Chesterfield. | Her last sickness | which was long & severe | she bore with all the patience & fortitude | which reason & religion could give | and continued intent on her devotions Till with her last breath on the 30th day of June 1752 | she recommended her soul into the hands of her Almighty Creator and Most Merciful Redeemer, To her Memory which will be ever honoured by and dear to him | this monument was erected by her most affectionate husband.

---

'North wall of chancel' :—

[ARMS.]

Near this place lie the remains of | Susanna Newcome | of the ancient family of the D'Oylys | Baronets in Oxfordshire | She married William Bishop of Dromore| and after the sharpest pain in childbirth | patiently breathed out her pure and pious soul to GOD | Dec, XXX, MDCCLXIX in the XXX year of her age.

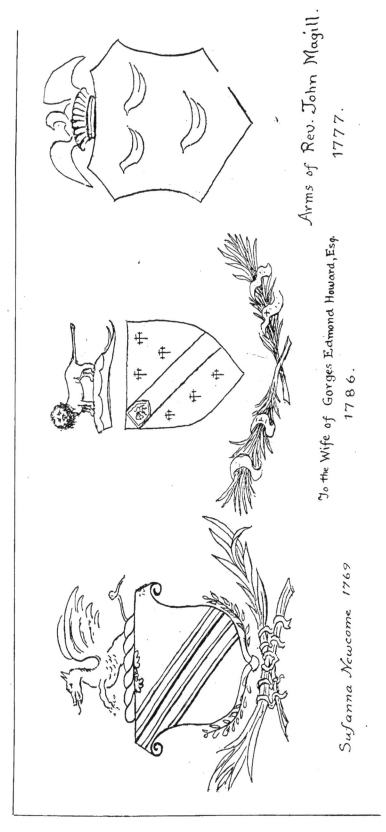

Arms of Rev. John Magill.
1777.

To the Wife of Gorges Edmond Howard, Esq.
1786.

Susanna Newcome 1769

**COATS-OF-ARMS ON TOMBSTONES IN ST. MARY'S CHURCH AND BURIAL-GROUND, DUBLIN.**

[*From drawings by Miss Eileen G. O'Mahony.*]

'In the north gallery' :—

[ARMS.]

Sacred to the memory of the Rev^d Robert Law, D.D. | Late Rector of this Parish, | of St Mary, | who departed this life June the 11^th 1789. | The parishioners of St. Mary's caused this monument to be erected, | in testimony of the high veneration and esteem | in which they ever held this truly excellent & beloved pastor | whose unremitting attention | during a period of seventeen years | To the Arduous & important offices of his station | whose faithful discharge of his various duties | and whose constant tender and pious zeal, | for their temporal and eternal welfare | Justly endeared him to the grateful affection of his whole flock | and whose afflicting loss, alas, will be long | severely felt by the poor | deeply regretted by the rich and sincerely lamented by all.

To the memory of M^r William Watson A.B., T.C.D., | he was respected as a citizen | amiable as a man & venerable as a Christian | In youth he was virtuous in manhood he was conscientious in advancing years he was exemplary | and earnest to be the Instrument of communicating that to others | which he found to be his own best security & truest happiness. | He conceived and shortly saw accomplished | the plan of an Association (now incorporated by Act of Parliament) for discountenancing vice | and Promoting the knowledge and Practise of the Christian Religion | the members of which body | desirous to express their gratitude | and prolong the influence of his example | have erected this monument | He departed this life 26^th May 1805 aged 72. | Reader, | Whatever be thy rank in life | thou will truly advance thyself by emulating the modest excellence | of William Watson.

To the beloved & honoured memory of | Isabella wife of | John M^cKenny | who departed this life the 12^th of July 1814 | in the 35^th year of her age | She was a Dutiful Daughter a loving wife | an affectionate Mother | and a sincere Friend. | She added to human virtue true piety | and having led a Christian life | she died in Christian triumph. | Her surviving husband erected this monument | In memory of her many virtues | and in gratitude for her conjugal & maternal love, | as a frail memorial of an imperishable affection.

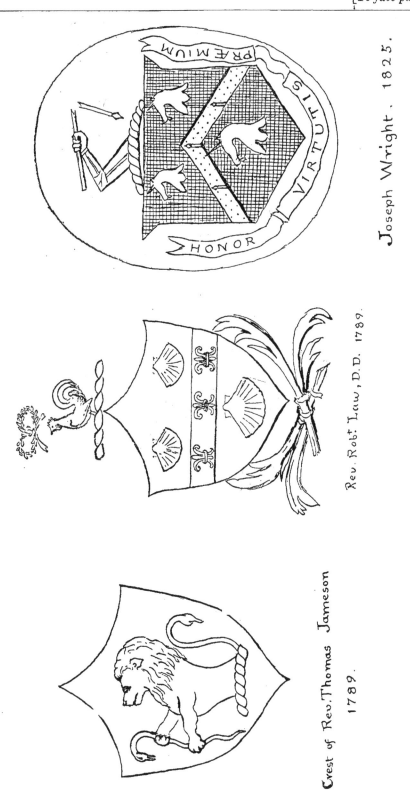

Crest of Rev. Thomas Jameson 1789.

Rev. Robt. Law, D.D. 1789.

Joseph Wright, 1825.

COATS-OF-ARMS ON TOMBSTONES IN ST. MARY'S CHURCH AND BURIAL-GROUND, DUBLIN.

[*From drawings by Miss Eileen G. O'Mahony.*]

' White marble tablet surmounted by an angel ':—

Obiit June 4<sup>th</sup> 1818 Æ 52. The members of | the Association for dis | countenancing vice | & promoting the knowledge and practise of | the Christian religion | have raised this last tribute to | William Watson | in grateful remembrance of | his long & unremitting devotedness | to all the objects & interests of the Association and | In testimony of | His personal virtue | which was genuine and unassuming | Liberal and conscientious | evincing itself | with exemplary uniformity | in every relation and transaction of life.

Sacred to the memory of | James Clarke Esq<sup>re</sup> M.D. | only son of Joseph and Isabella Clarke | of this City | who departed this life Oct 5<sup>th</sup> 1832 | This tablet is erected as a testimony of the | Devoted affection of his widow Margaret Clarke. | O tarry thou the Lord's leisure; be strong and He shall comfort thine heart; and put thou thy trust in the Lord.   Psa. 27 16.

Sacred to the memory of | Margaret | Daughter of the late Robert Stevelly Esq, of Cork |      wife of Thomas Wilson of Thorndale | County of Dublin, Esq<sup>re</sup> | in the bloom of youth | in the enjoyment of every | blessing which this world can bestow she was summoned | to the presence of her Creator; conscious of her situa- | tion and the inefficacy of all human aid; with the fortitude which is characteristic of the true Christian she | bade adieu to her friends, to her helpless and innocent children, to all she held most dear, and without a murmur resigned her gentle spirit to that Almighty Being | who gave it, | She was a sincere friend, a kind relation, a tender | and anxious mother and a most affectionate wife, | she died at Clifton, on the 10<sup>th</sup> of August 1822 | in the 26<sup>th</sup> year of her age.  Her remains are interred in the graveyard | attached to this church.

' In the south gallery ':—

[ARMS.]

Sacred | to the memory of Joseph Wright | of Duncairn in the County of Antrim | and Rutland Square West, Dublin, Solicitor | Who died 1<sup>st</sup> of June 1825 aged 57 years.  And of Mary his wife | who died 19<sup>th</sup> of March 1828 aged 59 years. | Lord, Thou wilt ordain peace for us, for Thou also hast wrought all our works in us. Isaiah 26 chap. 12 ver.

Near this spot lie the remains of | Francis Edmon-
stone | the first born son | of | Rev^d, Charles Bardin
A.M. | curate of St Mary's Parish. | He died on the 7^th
of April 1823 | an Infant | yet inexpressibly dear to his
Parents | Of such is the Kingdom of GOD.

---

Sacred to the memory | of the late William John Moore
Esq. | of Rutland Square | who departed this life
December the 28^th 1834 | in the 56^th year of his age. |
An affectionate husband, a Provident Parent | sincere
in his attachments | he lived | respected & beloved by
an extensive circle | of Friends and connexions | and
died in the fervent hope of ever lasting life | purchased
by the merits | and procured through the mediation |
of | our Blessed Lord and Saviour. | His grateful chil-
dren have caused this Tablet to be erected.

---

In testimony of sincere affection | this Tablet was
erected by | Ann Cave to the memory of her late brother
Richard Cave Esq^re | of North Frederick St. who died
4^th of August 1830 aged 80 years. | Beloved & esteemed
by all who knew him for strict integrity | & amiable
conduct through life his loss is now severely felt | He
was always ready to relieve the distressed | and in
justice may be said | he was a true & faithful servant
of his Saviour, | through whose merits alone he
departed | in hope of a joyful ressurrection. | Reader,
go and do thou likewise.

---

Near this are the remains of | John Allen and Alice his
wife | This stone is placed here by their sons | Richard
and John Allen | as a mutual token of grateful affec-
tion | in remembrance of the unceasing parental care |
and attention always shown them by their beloved &
regretted Father and Mother | Through all his life he
copyed Nature's plan | and as he lived so he died the
honest man. | She was a mother indeed and a truly
pious woman. | Interred in the same tomb with the
above named | John and Alice Allen | are the remains
of their eldest son | Richmond Allen | who departed
this life 3^rd July 1830. | aged 72 years. | In memory of
whom this tablet is inscribed | by his only & affec-
tionate brother.

' In a window splay of the north aisle ' :—

Sacred to the memory of | Sir John Riddell K$^t$. | who departed this life | 21$^{st}$ January 1831 | aged 67 years.

---

[ARMS.]

Sacred to the memory of Robert Morrison | who departed this life on the 16$^{th}$ day of March 1834 | in the 36$^{th}$ year of his age | Also to | Elizabeth his wife | who departed this life the 22$^{nd}$ of December 1842, | in the 30$^{th}$ year of her age. | This tablet is erected to their memory by their only child | Anna Maria Morrison.

---

This monument is erected | by Alderman Charles Carolin | of Lower Abbey Street Dublin to the memory of his | beloved wife, Anne Jane who departed this life in the joyful hope of a blessed Immortality | through Jesus Christ. | on the 1$^{st}$ of June 1838 | in the 36$^{th}$ year of her age | Lamented by all who knew her.

---

To, | the memory of | the Hon$^{ble}$ | Thomas Burton Vandeleur | Third Justice of | the Court of King's Bench | in Ireland | who died on the 14$^{th}$ of June 1835 | aged 66. | Jesus saith unto Martha | " Thy brother shall rise again " John ch. XI. v. 23. | Because I live, ye shall live also. John ch. XIV. v. 19.

---

' In the north aisle ' :—

[ARMS.]

Sacred to the memory of | the Rev$^d$, John Burdett | late of Rutland Square in | this City and for upwards of | 40 years Incumbent of the | United parishes of Rynagh and | Gallen in the diocese of Meath | as also of the Parish of | Ballygarth in the same diocese | died 5$^{th}$ of Sept$^r$ 1841 | in the 66$^{th}$ year of his age. | deeply regretted, This tablet is erected as the last tribute to his many virtues | and sterling worth.

---

Erected by the Parishioners & his private friends | to the memory of | the Rev$^d$, Hugh White A.M. | For 17 years curate of this parish | who died May 15$^{th}$ 1844. | aged 49 years. | Christianity found in him a no. less bright example than eloquent advocate. | The tendency and power of Gospel truth | to render the believer in

Jesus | holy and happy | were eminently displayed in his character and life | Constrained by the love of Christ | he laboured both in the pulpit and in private to win souls to Him. | and when lingering illness, endured without a murmur, no longer suffered him to speak in public | his pen was still employed in his beloved Masters service. " Thanks be to GOD for His unspeakable gift." 2 Cor. 9. 15.

To the memory of Michael Henry Whitestone Esq$^{re}$ Late of Hardwick St in this City. | who died the 16$^{th}$ of September 1845 aged 57 years | His mourning widow has caused this monument to be erected.

Near this lie the remains of | James Meredith James | who departed this life | 16$^{th}$ Sep$^r$ 1850 | also Mary his wife | on the 8$^{th}$ of Jan$^y$, 1855 | this tablet is erected by their four daughters. | as a sacred remembrance | of their deep & lasting love. | Do thou, O heaven | keep what thou hast taken | And with our treasure keep our hearts | on high | The spirit meek & yet by pain unshaken | The faith, the love, the lofty constancy | Guide us where these are with our parents flown. They were of Thee and Thou hast claimed Thine own. Let me die the death of the righteous and let my last end. be like theirs.

Sacred to the memory of M$^{rs}$. Susan Warren | Late of Great Charles Street in this City | who died on the 9$^{th}$ day of November 1858 | aged 66 years. | Also of Miss Margaret White sister of the above | who died on the 20$^{th}$ of August 1862, | aged 70 years.

In a vault underneath this church | are deposited the remains | of James Butler, Marquis of Ormonde, K.P. | Born 15$^{th}$ of July 1774 | and who departed this life | 22$^{nd}$ May 1838 | and of his two sons | Richard Molesworth Wandesforde Butler | born January 30$^{th}$ 1818 | died February 3$^{rd}$ 1838 | and Charles Wandesforde Butler | Lieut. R.N. | born February 7$^{th}$ 1820 | died October 30$^{th}$ 1857 | So teach us to number our days that we apply our hearts unto wisdom,
In the vault beneath the church | where lie the mortal remains of | her husband and her two sons | are also deposited those of Grace Louisa | Dowager Marchioness of Ormonde | who died May 3$^{rd}$ 1860 | aged 61 years.

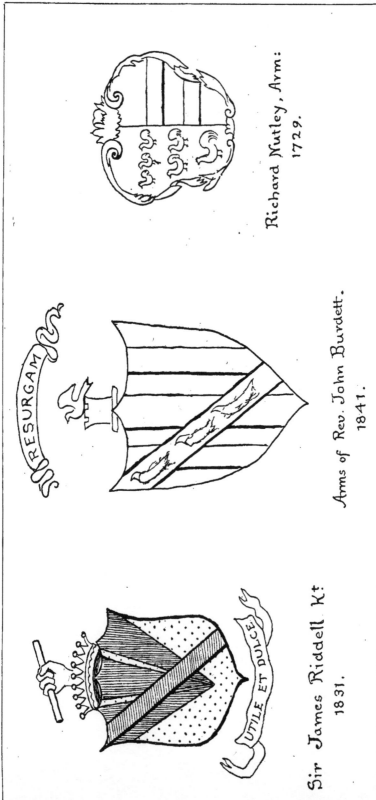

Richard Nutley, Arm: 1729.

RESURGAM

Arms of Rev. John Burdett. 1841.

Sir James Riddell Kt: 1831.

UTILE ET DULCE

**COATS-OF-ARMS ON TOMBSTONES IN ST. MARY'S CHURCH AND BURIAL-GROUND, DUBLIN.**

*From drawin     Miss Eileen G. O'Mahony.*]

Sacred | to the memory | of the Rev<sup>d</sup> John Black, M,A, | for 24 years Curate of this Parish | he entered into rest on the 7<sup>th</sup> of May 1883 | in the 54<sup>th</sup> year of his age | and the 31<sup>st</sup> of his ministry. | For what is our hope or joy, or crown of rejoicing? are not even ye in the presence of our LORD JESUS CHRIST at His coming. I Thess 2 c 19 v. | Erected in loving remembrance by the | Parishioners and other friends.

' On sides of monument ' :—

With Christ which is far better. Phil. I 23,
We have peace with GOD through our LORD JESUS CHRIST. Rom, 5. I.

----

' Memorial tablet on north side of chancel ' :—

[ARMS.]

M. S.

Richardi Nutley Armigeri
Sub Serenissima Anna
Unius Justiciariorum de Banco Regina
Viri
Qui in omni Officium genere
Quae vel utilem scient vel amabilem constituere
Feliciter et emicuit
In Literis Humanioribus Elegans & Perpositus* [sic]
In colloquis Comis & Urbanus
In Amicitijs Strenuus & Fidelis
In causis
Quas vel egerit Orator vel cognoverit Judex,
Gravis, Ornatus Perspicax Integerrimus
Tot interea Tantisq Negotijs Occupatus
In hoc unice Elaboravit
Ut Religioni ut Deo inserviret
Ut Vere Christianus semper audiret
Eo quippe adempto
Pauperes Refugium Certissimum,
Uxor Maritum Amantissimum,
Famuli Herum Benignissimum
Cognati (Quos in Liberorum loco habuit)
Parentum Alterum,
Optimum, Muniscientissimum
Deflent & Disiderant.
Ob. 10 Nov. 1729
Ætat 59

----

\* ? Præpositus.

' This last inscription has been contributed by the Rev. William Butler ; and a translation of it supplied by Miss Marjorie Carmichael Haywood, as follows ' :—

> Sacred to the memory of Richard Nutley, Esq., one of the Justices of the Queen's Bench under Her Most Serene Highness Anne. A man who excelled in every office both useful and friendly, skilled and foremost in the Arts and Sciences, urbane and courteous in speech, ready and faithful in Friendship, serious and eloquent, far-sighted and incorruptible whether pleading as a counsel or determining as a judge ; he was occupied also with many other matters of law. In all these he laboured effectually to serve God and His religion and to follow attentively the voice of Christianity. Yes, surely in him is lost the sure refuge for the poor, the most loving husband, the most benign master of a household ; those who were to him as children found in him a second parent, and him, the best, the most munificent, they bewail and mourn.

### Dublin, St. Michael's Church.
[From Mr. John Hewetson.]

'This church was taken down to give place for the present Synod Hall in St. Michael's Hill.

' When " Dyneley " visited it in 1681, he noted the following epitaph, which appeared in his manuscript " Tour in 1681," forming part of the library of Sir Thomas Winnington Ingram, Bart., Worcestershire, of which photographic reproductions are in the possession of John R. Garstin, Esq.' :—

> HERE LIETH THE BODY OF CAPTAIN THOMAS HEWETSON CAPTAIN OF A TROOP OF HORSE WHO WAS SLAYNE BY THE ENEMY IN THE PARLIAMENT SERVICE VI MAY MDCLI. DIED ABNER AS A FOOL DIETH ? THY HANDS WERE NOT BOUND NOR THY FEET PUT INTO FETTERS, AS A MAN FALLETH BEFORE WICKED MEN SO FELLEST THOU. SAM. II, 3, 23, 34. JUSTUS CADERE POTEST PERIRE NON POTEST.

*Crest* :—A Talbot passant holding in the mouth a sword.
*Arms* :—Hewetson empaling Smith, viz. :—

> For Hewetson : " Per pale ermine and gules, an eagle displayed or, charged on the breast with a crescent sable."
> For Smith : ? " Gules, three mullets pierced or, on a chief of the last as many pellets."

*Motto* :—Fidelis ad aras.

## Glasnevin Parish Churchyard,

[From Lord Walter FitzGerald.]

' The Patron Saint of Glasnevin was a St. Movee, who was venerated on the 2nd October. The Annals of the Four Masters thus record his death ' :—

" The age of Christ 544. Sᵗ. Mobhi "Claraineach" (i.e. of the flat face), i.e. Berchain, of Glais Naidhen on the brink of the Liffey, on the north side, died on the second day of the month of October."

' The oldest existing tombstone in the churchyard is a slab now fixed in the ground at the base of the church tower ; the inscription is incised, and reads ' :—

GEORGE CLAYTON DIED
IN MAY 1695 WALTER
FITZSIMONS DIED THE
10 OF IVNE 1699.

---

' The next oldest is a mural tablet, formerly in the south wall of the church, to which an aisle has recently been added, and now (May, 1909), it lies in many fragments at the east end of the church on the Barber table-tomb ; besides being in fragments, it is badly chipped, apparently owing to gross carelessness in its removal. The lettering is in large incised capitals, and with difficulty (when the pieces are put together) can be made out to run thus ' :—

REBVILT ANNO
DOMINI 1707
Sᴿ IOHN ROGERSON
[KNI]GHT AND CHARELS
   REEVES ESQᴿ
[C]HVRᶜH WARDENS

' This mural slab measured about 34 inches by 30 inches ; it commemorates the rebuilding of the church.'

---

' In the north-east corner of the churchyard there are two large mural slabs, in projecting frames, placed one above the other ; the lower one bears the following inscription ' :—

Here lyeth the Body of PATRICK DELANEY, D.D.
Formerly Senior Fellow of
Trinity College Dublin
Late Dean of Downe
An orthodox Christian Believer
An early & earnest Defender of Revelation

A constant & zealous Preacher of the Divine Laws
For more than fifty years,
And an humble Penitent
Hoping for mercy in Christ Jefus
He died the Sixth Day of May
MDCCLXVIII
In the Eighty-fourth year of his Age.

[See Miscellanea at the end of this Number.]

———

' The slab over the last-mentioned is of such an exceedingly bad quality that its surface has peeled off, leaving the inscription quite illegible except for a few words at the commencement of the lines; as far as can be deciphered they began thus ' :—

Here lyeth the Body . . . . . . . . .
D.D. and widow of . . . . . . . . .
A truly virtuous and . . . . . . . . .
four years with . . . . . . . . . .
And every f . . . . . . . . . . .
. . mittin . . . . . . . . . . .
Over . . . . . . . . . . . . .
A faithfull constant [gene] rous friend. A . . .
excellent Wife Mother Miſtreſs . . . . . .
A charitable compaſsi . . . . . . . . .
Blessed are the Peace makers for they . . . .
of God . . . . . . . . . . . .
Blessed are the [pure i] n spirit for . . . . . .
. . . . . . . . . . . . . . .

' Owing to the position of this slab, the lady must have been a connexion (? first wife)* of Dr. Delaney's ; it has every appearance of being much older than the slab of the latter, below it.'

———

' The inscriptions which follow are from some of the older tombstones in the churchyard, the majority of which were erected to the memory of Dublin tradesmen.'

' Headstones ranged along the east wall ' :—

This Stone and Burial | place Belongeth to | James Spencer of | pimlico Archell-maker | and his posterity 1740 | Here Lyeth two of | his children.

———

* Dr. Delaney, according to the " Dictionary of National Biography," was twice married ; first, in 1732 to a rich widow, Dame Margaret Tenison, who died on the 6th December, 1741 ; and secondly, in 1743 to Mary Granville, widow of Alexander Pendarves, who survived him, and died on the 15th April, 1788.

✝

## I H S

This Stone & Burial Place | Belongeth to John Connor of | S$^t$ Thomas Street linnen weave$^r$ | both for him & his Posterity | Jan$^{ary}$ y$^e$ 27$^{th}$ Anno Domino [sic] 1740 | Here Lyeth his Father & Mother | & 4 of his children

---

[CREST : A STAG.]
This Burial place belongs to M$^r$ | Ignatius Maguire of the City | of Dublin Merch$^t$ | Here lies the Body of his Brother | Rofs Maguire of s$^d$ City Merch$^t$ | who'departed this Life the 2$^{nd}$ of May | 1757 Aged 48 years | Also the Body of the above Igna$^s$ | Maguire who departed this life | Feb$^y$ 4$^{th}$ 1777 Aged 67 years likwise [sic] | 2 of his children who died yong [sic].

---

This Stone & Burial | Place Belongeth | To Rich$^d$ Houid & His | Posterity 1736 | Rich$^d$ Houid Died A$^{ugust}$ | y$^e$ 24$^{th}$ 1739 Aged 79.

---

✝

Cherub     I H S     Cherub
This Stone and burial place belongeth | to M$^r$ Rob$^t$ Hughes of the Barchelors walk | in the City of Dublin and his Posterity | Here lieth the body of M$^{rs}$ Ann Hughes | wife of the above Rob$^t$ Hughes who departed | this life the 9$^{th}$ of Feb$^y$ 1748 Aged 39 years | And also here lieth    of theire children | Also here lieth Interred [the rem]aines of the above | Robert Hughes wh[o depar]ted this life the 22$^{nd}$ | day of September [17   ] . . . . . . . year of his age.

---

✝

## I H S

This Stone and Burial Place bel | ongeth to John Mulvey of New | Row Shoemaker for himself and his | Posterity | Here lyeth the body of Francis | Mulvey who departed this life in | the year of our Lord 1750 aged | 60 years | Here lyeth the Body of the abo | ve named John Mulvey whome | this Stone was erected by, and he | departed this life Decem$^{ber}$ the 28$^{th}$ 1755 Aged  years.

'On the flaky headstone, on the south side of the chancel' :—

Skull and cross bones  I H S

Here lyeth y<sup>e</sup> Body of | John Long who Died | August y<sup>e</sup> 1<sup>st</sup> 1728, aged 58.

---

'Near the doorway of the new aisle' :—

I H S

This Stone and Burial Place | belongeth to Christopher M<sup>cc</sup> | Donaugh of Meath street in the | City of Dublin Dyer and his | Posterity 1739 | Here lyeth 4 of his children | Requiescant in Pace.

---

'On a large headstone facing the west' :—

Gloria in Excelsis Deo

Memen<sup>to</sup>    I H S    mori

This Stone and burial place
belongs to Mary Geraty and her
posterity.  her<sup>e</sup> lieth the Remains
of the Rev<sup>d</sup> W<sup>m</sup> Reily who
Dep<sup>d</sup> this life June the 11<sup>th</sup> 1779
Aged 90 years.
Here lieth the body of
Mary Geraghty of Leixlip
who departed the 11<sup>th</sup> of Feb<sup>y</sup> 1819.

---

'Broken headstone' :—

This . . . . . . .
Place belong . . . . .
Sauage of Church St . . . .
and his Posterity who . . . .
Parted this Life the 31 . . .
August 1716, and in t . . .
54<sup>th</sup> year of his age.

---

'On a flat slab at the foot of the above' :—

This Stone and Burial Place belongeth
to Peter Sauage late of Smithfield
& his posterity who departed this
life Decemb<sup>r</sup> the 8<sup>th</sup> 1755 aged 35 years
& Erected by his wife Margret Sauage.

' On the south side of the churchyard ' :—

I H S

This Stone and Burial Place | Belongeth to Iames Spencer | of Pimblico Archell maker an<sup>d</sup> | his Posterity who Departed | this Life the 9<sup>th</sup> of Nov<sup>r</sup> 1746 | aged 43 years | Here Lyeth three of his childr<sup>en</sup> | Elenor Margrett and Benjamin | Here also Lyeth the Body of | Ellenor O'Neall of Pimblico | Mother of the above, who Dep | arted this Life the 23<sup>rd</sup> day of Feb | ruary 1750 aged 75 years.

---

I H S

THIS STONE & BURIAL | PLACE BELONGS TO PAT | RI<sup>C</sup>K BYRN & HIS POSTERITY | HERE LIS (*sic*) Y<sup>E</sup> BODY OF Y<sup>E</sup> S<sup>D</sup> P.B. | WHO DECEASED IANUARY Y<sup>E</sup> 17<sup>TH</sup> | 1729.  AGED 43 YEARS.

---

This | Stone and Burial place be | longeth to M<sup>r</sup> Simon Luneman | Gen<sup>t</sup> who departed this life | Oct<sup>r</sup> y<sup>e</sup> 1<sup>st</sup> 1748 Aged 24 years

---

' On a thick headstone of red sandstone ' :—

+

Cherub    I H S    Cherub

Gloria in Excelsis Deo

This Stone and Burial Place Belongeth
to Michael M<sup>cc</sup>Cormuck of Church Street,
Dealer, and to his Posterity.
And also here lieth the Body of his Father
Patrick M<sup>cc</sup>Cormuck who departed this life
the 17<sup>th</sup> day of November 1749 Aged 55 years.
And also here lieth the Body of his Mother
Allice M<sup>cc</sup>Cormuck who departed this life
the 18<sup>th</sup> day of April 1768 Aged 72 years
And 3 of their children.  Requiescant in Pace
Amen

'On the west side of the churchyard' :—

'Square headstone' :—

✝

Skull      I H S      Crossbones

HERE LYETH THE BODY OF | HENERY FOORD OF KINGS S | TREET PARISH OF SAINT | MICHANS WHO DEPART | ED THIS LIFE THE NINTH | DAY OF IVNE 1743 IN | THE SIXTY<sup>TH</sup> YEAR OF HIS | AGE. THIS STONE WAS | ERECTED BY HIS WIFE BR | IDGET FOORD FOR TH | ERE POSTERETY HERE LY | ETH ALSO NINE OF |

[Remainder underground]

---

'On a square headstone' :—

Here lyeth the Body of Henry | Dickenson who departed this | Life February the 25<sup>th</sup> 1751 aged 72.

'On the top edge of this stone is cut' :—

Ben. Iackson of Liffey Street Dubli<sup>n</sup>.

---

'Square headstone' :—

HERE UNDER LIETH THE
BODY OF ELIZABETH TAAFFE
ALIAS RYLY THE WIFE OF GEORGE
TAAFFE OF DUBLIN BAKER WHO
DECEASED THE 22 DAY OF IUNE
17. .

---

'On a headstone in the south-east corner' :—

Here lyeth y<sup>e</sup> Body of M<sup>r</sup> Rich<sup>d</sup>
Bolton who died Feb<sup>y</sup> y<sup>e</sup> 15<sup>th</sup> 1722
Aged 51 years & Eliz<sup>th</sup> his Wife
who died Jan<sup>y</sup> 1<sup>st</sup> 1734 Aged 63 ye

'The remainder of this inscription is hid by a flat Bolton slab at the foot of the headstone.'

---

'Lying in the pathway, near the vestry, is a flat slab, bearing this inscription' :—

Here lieth the Body of the Rev<sup>d</sup> John
Boyle, A.M., who was Minister of this
Parish for 25 years, he died the 4<sup>th</sup> of
Dec<sup>r</sup> 1779 Aged 72 years.

'Inside the church, on the west wall, is a mural marble monument thus inscribed ' :—

SUBTER IN CRYPTA
REQUIESCANT
ANDREAS GULIELMI CALDWELL FILIUS AMICUS
NAT. 1683 OB. 1731.
ET
HUGO ANDREÆ FILIUS NATU MINIMUS
NAT. 1708 OB. 1710
HOC MONUMENTUM PIETATIS CAUSA
CAROLUS BENJAMIN CALDWELL
ET
SOPHIA FRANCES CUST
UXOR DILECTISSIMA
POSUERUNT
A.D. 1871.

' On a brass, at the base of this monument, there is a shield, bearing two coats-of-arms impaled, each of them quartered.
' On a scroll is inscribed in black-letter ' :—

Ense Liberta | tem Petit | Inim | ico Tyrannis.

## Howth Abbey Burial-ground.

[From Lord Walter FitzGerald.]

' Most of the inscriptions from this burial-ground were copied by Miss Vize, and appeared on pages 194–7, 373–8 of the fifth volume of the JOURNAL. The following two inscriptions, however, escaped her notice ' :—

' On a headstone at the south side ' :—-

HERE LIETH THE
BODY OF RICH$^D$
NEALAND WHO
DEPARTED THIS
LIFE NOV$^R$ Y$^E$ 16$^{TH}$
1735.

' On a leaning-inwards headstone in the north aisle ' :—

+
I. H. S

This Stone was Erected by Martin | Coats of Clontarf Over the Remains | of his Brother Richard Coats who | departed this life the 3$^{rd}$ of March | 1764 Aged 56 years. | Also his niece Mary Roork who | departed this life the 4 of April. [The remainder is underground.]

'On page 377 some ten or twelve more lines of inscription on the table-tomb of the Clarke family follow, but they are quite illegible.

'On page 374 is given the inscription on Patrick Duggan's tombstone, which consists of a flat slab, badly fractured. The date is broken across, but I read it 1810.'

---

'On the south side of the burial-ground, now being used as a headstone, is an ancient slab on which is sculptured a cross in relief, the terminals of which end in fleurs-de-lys.'

---

## Kilbarrack Churchyard.

### [From Lord Walter FitzGerald.]

'The ruins of Kilbarrack Church stand near the sea-shore by the side of the public road leading from Dollymount to the Sutton and Baldoyle Railway Station. They consist of a nave and chancel, and had a south aisle. The south wall of the aisle and the whole of the west end of the ruins are down. The remains contain no cut-stone work. The oldest tombstone in the burial-ground does not date earlier than 1728.

'The following four inscriptions are the oldest that I could discover.

'On a large, rough headstone':—

✝
I. H. S

Here lieth the Body of Tho<sup>s</sup> | Ash who departed this Life D<sup>r</sup> | y<sup>e</sup> 25 1755. Aged 44 y<sup>rs</sup>. This Stone | is erected by his wife Mary | Ash for themselves and their Po | sterity.

---

'On a flat slab':—

✝
I. H. S
Here lyeth the Body of the Reverend
Father Nicholas Sweetman who departe<sup>d</sup>
this life the 26<sup>th</sup> December 1741 aged 28
years.
Also lyeth Here the Body of Christopher
Sweetman who departed this life the
22<sup>nd</sup> June 1746. Aged 35 years
This Stone and Buriall place Belongeth
to Thomas Sweetman of Killorrock [sic] for
him and the use of his Posterity.

' On a headstone ' :—

+
I. H. S

Here lyeth the Body of | Frances Sweetman | alias
Wade who departed | this life the  –7 of March | 1728
Aged 47 years | This Stone was Erected | by John
Sweetman of | Larkhill for him and | his Posterity.

---

' On a flat slab ' :—

This Stone & Burial place | belongs to Patrick
Sweetman | of the City of Dublin, Brewer & his |
Posterity.  Here lyes the Body of M$^{rs}$ Cath$^{n}$ Browne
Als. Sweetman | who departed this life the 28 day |
of Feb$^{y}$ 1747-8 in the 20$^{th}$ year of | her age | Here also
lyeth the Body of | Patrick Sweetman of S$^{t}$ | Stephen's
Green in the City of | Dublin who departed this | Life
January the 1$^{st}$ 1770 Aged | 68 years. | Here also lies
interred the Body of | Mary Sweetman of Foxhall wife |
to the above Patrick Sweetman who depar | ted this life
on the 8$^{th}$ day of September 1784 | Aged 92 years |
Requiescant in pace Amen.

---

' On a flat slab outside the east window ' :—

Here lyes the Body of
M$^{r}$ James Fottrill And al
so the Body of his son John
Fottrill who departed this
life the 18 day of May 1732 Aged
52 years.
Likewise the Body of Elenor
Fottrill daughter of John
who departed this life July
the 30$^{th}$ 1751 Aged 25 years.
This Stone is Erected by M$^{rs}$
Anabell Fottrill of Foxhall.

---

## Kilcrea Churchyard, Parish of Donabate.

[From Lord Walter FitzGerald.]

This churchyard lies by the roadside a mile to the south of
Donabate.  It is in a disgraceful state of neglect.  The ditch
surrounding it is full of gaps, giving free access to cattle.  Rabbits
burrow among the neglected graves, and timber felled by the storm

of 1903 has not yet been removed. Of the ruins of the old church
the east gable still stands, and a good portion of the north and
south walls still exist. The west end is down. There is no window
in the north wall. In the south wall are the remains of the doorway
and of a window. No cut-stone work remains, and the east window
is a mere gap in the wall.

'Though rough stones mark the position of many graves, there
is only one headstone bearing a lightly incised inscription, which
reads as follows ' :—

Here Lieth the Body
Of Iames Fitzgearld [*sic*] Died 18 Nov<sup>r</sup> 1777
Aged 36 years.

'The church was a small one. Externally it measures 17 feet
9 inches in breadth, 30 feet in length, and the walls are 2 feet 4
inches thick.'

---

### Killossery Churchyard.

[From Mr. J. R. Fowler.]

✝

IHS

This Stone and burial place belong to Tho<sup>s.</sup> Kettle and
his Pofterity Anno Domini 1792 here lieth the body of
his Father Patt<sup>k.</sup> Kettle who departed this life

(Rest below ground.)

---

✝

IHS

This Stone & Burying place Belongeth to Andrew
Barnewell July 30th 1773  Here lyeth the body of the
above

(Rest below ground.)

---

✝

Memento IHS Mori

This Stone and Burial Place belongeth to M<sup>r</sup> William
Rogers and his Pofterity  Here Lyeth the Body of y<sup>e</sup>
above Said William Rogers who Departed this Life the
24<sup>th</sup> of August 1742 Aged 64 years here alfo Lyeth the
Body of his Wife Ann Rogers and four of their
Children

✠
This  I H S  Stone

was erected here by Andrew Kenny of Baleuruy in memory of his Son Patt^k Kenny who departed this life the 6^th of January 1791 aged 25 years.

---

Luke O'Reilly of Lispoppel 23^rd Dec 1821.

---

I H S.

The Buriall place of Will^m | Connell who departed | this life the 8^th of Decemb^r | 1717  Aged 55 years | also his wife Agnis Conne^ll | alias Kenedy the sam be | ing directed by his Son | Richard . . . . . .
(Rest under ground.)

---

This Stone and burial | Place belongeth to | . . . . Banister | here Lyeth y^e body of | . . . . Banister | who departed this | Life y^e 7^th of Novemb | 1721 ag^ed 64 years |

---

This stone Belongeth to James . Caerthy of Rebate here lieth his Wife Mary Who died July 6 1769 Aged 60 years .

---

✠
I H S

Erected by Patrick Cuffe of Swords to his Wife & 3 Children 30 Sept 1800 also above named P. Cuffe died 27 April 1829

---

✠
I H S
(cherub)                    (cherub)

Erected by Margaret Grimes to her husband Richard Grimes died 8^th Feb 1822 aged 34 also her brothers Michael & Henry Charles and 3 children John, Andrew, Mary Anne

Gloria in Excelsis Deo

✝

Memento I H S Mori

Thomas Brangan of Swords and family Mrs Catherine
Brangan died 8th Dec 1772 Aged 42 & 2 of his Children
John and Judith with 15 of his grandchildren who died
young and his Daughter in law Mary Brangan 6th Dec
1798 aged 28 & Laurence Brangan died 27 Feb 1827
aged 76   Christopher Brangan died 25 Jan 1800 and
his Wife Catherine died 1804

---

✝

(cherub)   I H S   (cherub)

Henry O'Brien for him and his posterity A.D. 1809.

---

Agnus Dei

Michael Cuffe of Swords died 9 July 1848 aged 52
and brother Thomas Cuffe of Lissenhall 19th Oct 1851
aged 58 Sarah Wife of Michael Cuffe died Palm
Sunday 1876

---

### Malahide Churchyard.

[From Mr. V. Hussey-Walsh.]

Here lies the body of Maria Catherine Henley
Wife of Michael Henley Esq
of La Mancha near this Cemetery
She was prematurely taken from her numerous and weeping family
of whose love and veneration
She was deservedly the object ; in the fiftieth year of her age
On the 22nd day of November 1819
Here also lies the body of Mary Harney
Her mother
Who departed this life in the 69th year of her age
On the 2nd of August 1819
May the Almighty God be gracious to their Souls
Here lieth the body of
Michael Henley Esqre
late of La Mancha
He was born on the 11th of November 1766
And died on the 22nd February 1825
In the 59th year of his age

· He was a bright, wise and excellent man
Whose actions were characterized by probity
And words by truth
And whose chief enjoyment
During a life of sedulous industry
Was the sedulous contemplation of the happiness
Which as benefactor friend and father
He was ever employed in creating around him.
May he rest in Peace   Amen

---

## EXPLANATORY PEDIGREE.

HENRY HENLEY, of Malahide, Co. Dublin, mar 1st . . . ?
by whom he had issue :—

1. Michael, who follows

2. Thomas, b. 1780, mar. Anne Carmody and died in Paris
   21st Feb. 1828.  His widow died in Paris 2nd March
   1828.  She made will 28th Feb., probate· 26th Sept.
   1828.

3. James.

He married secondly Margaret Gillespie, and died 23rd April
1810, leaving issue by this marriage :—

1. John, b. 1803, d. 24th April 1825.

2. William, b. 1804, made a will 16th Aug. 1825.  Adminis-
   tration granted with will annexed 8th Sept. 1826.

MICHAEL HENLEY, b. 11th Nov. 1766 ; mar. Maria  Catherine
(b. 1769, d. 22nd Nov. 1819 ; tombstone inscription at Malahide),
dau. of Martin Savage, by his marriage with Mary Cotter, who
married secondly — Harney, of 9 Henry Street, Dublin (M. I.
Malahide), and died 22nd Feb. 1825, leaving issue :—

1. Thomas Henry, LL.D., T.C.D., b. 1790, d. at New York
   Aug. 27, 1835.

2. Michael, b. 1800, Ensign Bedfordshire Regt. 24th May
   1824 ; Captain, 28th Jan. 1826 ; died 1840.

3. Charles, b. 1803, Ensign 44th Regt. 12th Sept. 1816 ;
   M.D. Louvain Univ., Belgium, 7th April 1827 ; died
   4th Jan. 1828 ; tombstone inscription at Malahide, see
   JOURNAL, vol. iii, p. 443.

4. John Joseph Henley, b. 9th Decr 1809 ; mard 10th Jany 1839
   Narcissa Jane dau. of Thomas Molton of Montgomery,

Alabama, U.S.A. (she was born 4$^{th}$ Dec$^r$ 1824, and d. 3$^{rd}$ April 1900), leaving issue :—

(1) Thomas Molton Henley, b. 3 Dec$^r$ 1839 ; mar$^d$ at Randolph, Alabama, U.S.A., 11$^{th}$ July 1876, Alcesta dau. of Malcolm Currie Smith by Mary, dau. of Daniel Watson of Randolph, Alabama ; he d. 4$^{th}$ April 1888, leaving issue : —

    1. Mary Narcissa, b. 17$^{th}$ May 1877.
    2. Robert Hestor, b. 4$^{th}$ Feb$^y$ 1879.
    3. Annie Olivia, b. 29$^{th}$ May 1881.
    4. Lettice Jane, b. 27$^{th}$ Dec$^r$ 1883.
    5. Thomas Molton, b. 6$^{th}$ April 1886.
    6. Malcolm John, b. 23$^{rd}$ June 1888, d. 29$^{th}$ April 1890.

(2) John Charles Henley of Birmingham, Alabama, b. 29$^{th}$ Sep$^r$ 1842 ; mar$^d$ 25$^{th}$ Jan$^y$ 1876 Annie dau. of Charles Linn of Stockholm, Sweden (by Charlotte Antoinette dau. of Walter Fores), and widow of William Van Buren Matthews of Louisville, Kentucky (who d. 11$^{th}$ March 1871) ; he died 15$^{th}$ May 1909, leaving issue :—

    1. Walter Ervine, b. 31$^{st}$ Jan$^y$ 1877.
    2. John Charles, b. 9$^{th}$ Oct$^r$ 1880 ; mar$^d$ in Memphis, Tennessee, Lamira dau. of Robert A. Parker (by Lamira Minter dau. of Uriah G. Berry) on the 26$^{th}$ April 1906, and had issue :—
        (a) Lamira Charles, b. 27$^{th}$ Nov$^r$ 1908.
        (b) Edmonia Berry, b. 17$^{th}$ July 1910 (?)
    3. Courtney Scott, b. 20$^{th}$ Dec$^r$ 1890.

(3) Michael Henry Henley, b. 18$^{th}$ March 1844 ; d. 19$^{th}$ May 1854.

(4) Robert Walton Henley, b. 11$^{th}$ Aug$^t$ 1850 ; d. 9$^{th}$ Jan$^y$ 1864.

(1) Catherine, b. 22 Feb$^y$ 1841 ; d. 9$^{th}$ Sep$^t$ 1842.

(2) Narcissa Jane, b. 28$^{th}$ July 1846 ; d. 12$^{th}$ Nov$^r$ 1848.

(3) Anna Julia, b. 16$^{th}$ March 1848 ; d. 6$^{th}$ July 1849.

1. Maria, b. 25th Feb. 1791, baptized at St. Michan's, Halston Street, Dublin, 3rd March 1791 ; mar. at La Mancha, 18th Aug. 1817, John Hussey Walsh, Esq., of

Kilduff, King's County (brother of Walter Walsh ; tombstone inscription at Malahide), and died at Kilduff, King's County, 14th May 1869.

2. Elizabeth, b. 20th April 1795 ; d. at Fontainebleau, France, 12th Jan. 1875.

3. Frances, b. 20th May 1800 ; mar. in Dublin, March, 1832, John, son of Denis Sampson, Esq., and died at Boulogne-sur-Mer, France, 15th October 1872.

4. Anna, b. 1807, d. at Fontainebleau, France, 11th Feb. 1872.

5. Catherine, b. 1809, d. 1840.

6. Letitia Olivia, bapt. 11th Nov. 1811, at La Mancha, County Dublin ; d. at Castellamare, Italy, 14th June, 1884.

Here lyeth the body of Walter Walsh Esq the youngest brother of John Hussey Walsh of Mount Hussey County of Roscommon   He was beloved whilst he lived for he possessed many estimable qualities but was chiefly remarkable for sweetness of disposition, piety of morals, benevolence of heart & disinterested rectitude of purpose He died sincerely lamented in the 21$^{st}$ year of his age on the 29$^{th}$ of June 1818.   May Almighty God be gracious to his Soul

## Monkstown Church, Co. Dublin.

[From Mrs. T. Long.]

Sacred to the memory of Benjamin Domville D.D. who was born May 19$^{th}$ 1711 and died Oct$^r$ 18$^{th}$ 1774. He entertained the deepest sense of the importance and exerted the most conscientious diligence in the discharge of his sacred office, his discourses addressed to the understanding and the heart were so powerfully enforced by animated language and strength of reasoning, that he was justly admired as the most persuasive preacher of his time.   Equally respected in private life, his filial piety, conjugal affection and tender regard to all his family, were most exemplary.   Invariable in friendship, unbounded in benevolence, the great object of his constant endeavours was to promote the honour of God and the happiness of mankind.   This humble monument was erected by his grateful and afflicted Widow.

Inscribed to the memory of Lieut. General James Stewart Late Lt. Col. of His Majesties 5<sup>th</sup> or Royal Irish Reg<sup>t</sup> of Dragoons who departed this life in Dublin 1<sup>st</sup> of May 1798 aged 58 years. Much honoured and lamented by Miss Jane Stewart his beloved Daughter. This monument is erected by Major Maxwell of the 7<sup>th</sup> Dragoon Guards the nephew and late Aid-de-Camp to the General in token of their love and regard.

---

[From Monkstown Register. Printed by Parish Register Society.]

## SUCCESSION OF CLERGY FROM 1630-1800.

| | | |
|---|---|---|
| 1630. Thomas Lloyd Morris | ... ... | Curate in Charge. |
| 1639. Thomas Davis ... | ... ... | Curate. |
| 1642. Randolph Foxtwist. | | |
| 1670. Thomas Ward ... | ... ... | Do. |
| 1685. William Deāne ... | ... ... | Do. |
| 1691. Alan Maddison ... | ... ... | Do. |
| 1740. Daniel Dickinson | ... ... | Curate Assistant. |
| 1742. Thomas Heany ... | ... ... | Curate. |
| 1762. Henry Wright ... | ... | Curate Assistant. |
| 1768. Alexander La Nauze | ... ... | Do. |
| 1769. Thomas Robinson | ... ... | Curate. |
| 1770. John Andrews ... | ... ... | Curate Assistant. |
| 1773. Isaac Ashe ... | ... ... | Do. |
| 1775. John Healy ... | ... | Curate. |
| 1775. Edward Beatty ... | .. | Curate Assistant. |
| 1779. Edward Ledwich | .. ... | Curate. |
| 1780. John Forsayeth ... | ... ... | Do. |
| 1782. William Jephson | ... ... | Do. |
| 1785. John Burrowes ... | ... ... | Curate Assistant. |
| 1791. John William Ryves | ... ... | Curate. |
| 1792. Robert Burrowes | ... ... | Curate Assistant. |
| 1798. Marmaduke Cramer | ... ... | Curate. |
| 1799. George Robinson | ... ... | Curate Assistant. |

---

## Newcastle Lyons Churchyard,

[From Mr. T. U. Sadleir.]

These are supplemental to the inscriptions published in vol. vi.'

This stone and burial place belongeth to Peter Barnewall, and his posterity. Likewise to his wife Margaret Moor 1763. Likewise lyeth Hear three of his children.

. . . ter Braughall, who dyed July the 28$^{th}$ 1721.

---

This stone was erected by James Condren, of Brabazon
. . . , Dublin, in memory of his wife . . . Condren,
who departed this life . . . 1797, aged 46. Also her
daughter Mary Anne Lawler.

---

Erected by Peter Connolly in memory of his beloved
wife Catherine Connolly, who departed this life October
3$^{rd}$ 1828, aged 72 years. Also his mother Mary
Connolly who departed this life . . . 1790, aged 85
years.

---

' Altar-tomb, railed in ' :—

Beneath this stone are deposited the remains of Pierrepoint Oliver Mitchell Esq. who departed this life on the
7$^{th}$ March 1835, in the 53$^{rd}$ year of his age. To his
friends his memory is his best epitaph.
His nephew John Tottenham Langrishe Esq has erected
this memorial of him as a token of his regard, and in
testimony of his gratitude.

Here lieth also the body of Mary Harriet sister of the
above named Pierrepoint Oliver Mitchell, who departed
this life on the . . . of August 1842. Also that of her
beloved husband the Ven. James Langrishe, Archdeacon
of Glendalough, who died on 17$^{th}$ March 1847, aged 82.

John Tottenham Langrishe died 1888, aged 79.
Anna Maria Langrishe died 1898, aged 75.

---

Erected by Thomas Cantfil in memory of his father
James Cantfil, who departed this life June 4$^{th}$ 1790, aged
72 years. Also Maurice Cantfil, his brother, who
departed this life . . . 1794, aged 27 years. Also
Martin Cantfil, who departed this life August 26$^{tb}$ 1798,
aged 19 years.

---

' Altar-tomb ' :—

Here lieth the Body of Richard Morgan Esq, Departed
this life September 25$^{th}$ 1786, aged 70 years.

' This was the founder of Morgan's Endowed Schools at
Castleknock. For this purpose he devised considerable landed
property to trustees ; but the will being contested, by his nephew

and heir-at-law, John Godley, of Pearmount, Co. Dublin, only half
the estate eventually became available for the charity. When
first opened, the school was housed in what is now Rathcoole
Rectory.'

Catherine Ryan in memory of her beloved husband
Mr Patrick Ryan, Corn Chandler, late of Thomas Street,
in the City of Dublin . . . the 21st of May 1803 in the
49th year of his age: Here also lieth two of their
children William and Mary Ryan.

This stone was erected by Anne Kelly in memory of her
husband Patrick Kelly, who departed this life June 7th
1803, aged 55 years.

' There is a large vault in one corner of the churchyard, but
Mr. Fowler is wrong in supposing that it bears no inscription.
Had he examined the large stone placed over the doorway, he would
have found the following ' :—

Erected by John Keogh, of Loughlinstown, County of
Kildare, Esq. in the year of our Lord one thousand eight
hundred and one.

' A pedigree of this family will be found in Burke's " Visitation
of Seats and Arms." They lived in a house half-way between
Hazelhatch Station and St. Wolstan's, and of which little trace now
exists.'

Here lieth the body of Neason Augustine Coyne, who
departed this life the 5th of January 1829, Aged 19
years.
He was a pious virtuous youth, as a son and brother
he may be equalled by many, but exceeded by none.
This stone was erected by his loving mother to his
memory.

# MISCELLANEA.

## The Bethesda Church, Dorset Street, Dublin.

*Extract from a Daily Paper of the 7th March, 1911* :—

" The alteration of the Bethesda Church to suit it for its new purpose is being rapidly carried out. A new flooring is to be laid down, and a large part of the basement has been excavated. *A number of memorial tablets which were on the walls when the building was used as a place of worship have been removed*, and all the fittings of the church have been taken away. The Cinematograph Company, which has secured a lease for a long term from the trustees of the church, have posters on the wall announcing that as soon as the alterations are completed there will be continuous performances at the Picture Theatre, and that teas, &c., will be provided. The change of the building to its new purpose will alter in a very considerable degree the aspect of what is at present one of the quietest and at nightfall one of the worst-lighted portions of Dorset Street."

['What has become of the memorial Tablets ?'—EDITOR.]

## The Glasnevin Parish Church Enlargement, 1908.

*Extract from the " Irish Times " of the 14th December, 1908* :—

" On Thursday, December 17th, a function of more than ordinary interest to the parishioners of Glasnevin will take place, in connexion with their ancient and historic parish church, when His Grace the Archbishop will dedicate the new aisle, which has been built at a cost of £850, and which constitutes a very necessary addition to the hitherto inadequate seating accommodation. It must be a source of extreme satisfaction to all interested in the project, that the work now completed leaves little to be desired, the smallest detail having been submitted to anxious and careful consideration. The result which has been achieved within the comparatively short period of six months by the parishioners of Glasnevin, aided by some generous friends outside the parish, is a most gratifying one, and will remain as a permanent memorial of their zeal. It may not be out of place here to mention a few facts of interest connected with the old parish of Glasnevin. The history of the parish dates back to the time of St. Mobhi, who died in the year 544. The old church is still associated with his name as its founder. St. Mobhi was the head of a religious community numbering about fifty scholars, who lived in huts on the banks of the Tolka, just where the Botanic Gardens are now situated. Here it was that St. Columba came to finish his education, before he founded the abbey at Durrow, as well as other churches, and later on left Ireland for Iona. The old church of St. Mobhi was restored many times during past centuries. Of one rebuilding, which took place in the year 1707, when the whole church was restored, with the exception of the tower, which remains as it was before that date, we have an exact account in an existing parochial record. Dean Swift often came to Glasnevin to visit his intimate friends, Dean and Mrs. Delany. It would appear that Dr. Delany acted for some years as incumbent of Glasnevin. He lived at Delville, a fine residence adjoining the church grounds, into which there is a private entrance, referred to by Mrs. Delany in her ' Memoirs.'* Swift's celebrated ' Drapier's Letters ' are believed to have been printed at Delville. The tomb of Dr. J. Barrett, the learned, though eccentric, Vice-Provost of T.C.D., as well as the reputed site of Robert Emmet's burial-place, can be seen in the churchyard. Just eleven years ago, a chancel was added to this old historic church, which considerably increased the number of pews available for the congregation, as well as for the choir. In consequence, however, of the steady influx of population to this suburban district of Dublin, it was found needful to obtain further accommodation. Hence the present enlargement, which has taken the form of an aisle on the south side of the church. This aisle opens into the old portion by a row of graceful arches, which support the existing roof. The new aisle is about thirteen feet wide, inside measurement, and extends the whole length of the church, about sixty feet, while the area of the organ chamber has been also considerably increased, and thus adapted to the accommodation of a larger instrument than that at present in use. Much credit is due to the architects, Messrs. W. M. Mitchell and Son, by whom the plans were drawn up, and also to Messrs. B. Pemberton and Sons, contractors, for the manner in which the work has been executed."

---

* See pp. 315, 316, for Dr. Delany's tombstone inscription.

# NOTES.

## James Napper Tandy.

The following correspondence in connexion with this '98 leader appeared in the *Irish Times* in March, 1907 :—

JAMES NAPPER TANDY.

SIR,—While collecting materials for the history of this parish, I have come across an inscription on a flat tombstone in the parish churchyard at Castle Bellingham which runs as follows :—

"Under lies the body of Hen. Hughes, of Castle-bellingham, Esq., died 10th March, 1792 ; also his grandson, James Napper Tandy ; also his wife, Mary Hughes, died 1802."

I am anxious to know if this refers to James Napper Tandy of '98 fame. Perhaps some of your readers can throw some light on the matter. James Napper Tandy, I believe, died at Bordeaux in 1803. Were his remains brought to Castle Bellingham ? I have made inquiries from several who, as I thought, should have information to solve this question, but no one, as yet, has been able to give me any definite answer.

There is no doubt that the Hughes and Tandy families were connected. The Tandy family seems also to have intermarried with the Bellinghams.

I am inclined to believe— unless any of your readers can show cause otherwise—that the Tandy of the inscription was the rebel, and that for two reasons :—

1. The paucity of information about him on the tombstone—where the date of his death is not even given—suggests it.

2. I have never heard of another of the same name, living at, and dying about the same time.—Yours, &c.,

JAMES B. LESLIE, M.A., Clk.

SIR.—In reply to the Rev. J. B. Leslie's letter of inquiry, *re* James Napper Tandy, of '98 fame, which appeared in your issue of the 11th inst., the following will, I expect, help to clear up the difficulty :—

James Tandy, merchant, of Dublin, seventh son of John Tandy, of Drewstown, Co. Meath, Esq., married, in 1731, Maria Bella Jenkins, and had by her three children, viz. :—(1) James Napper

Tandy, of '98 fame ; (2) George Tandy, of Lisburn ; and (3) Anne, married George Wilkinson, Esq., of Limerick.

James Napper Tandy had an only son, James, who was married in October, 1788, at Castle Bellingham, to Miss Hughes, only daughter of Henry Hughes, Esq., of that place.

As the James Napper Tandy mentioned on the tombstone is stated to have been a grandson of Henry Hughes, of Castle-bellingham, he must have been a son of the above-mentioned Lieutenant James Tandy and Miss Hughes, and therefore a grandson of James Napper Tandy, of '98 fame, who died at Bordeaux in 1803, aged 63.

With regard to the Bellingham-Tandy relationship, Anne Tandy, daughter of Edward Tandy, merchant, of Dublin (fourth son of the above John Tandy, of Drewstown, County Meath, Esq.), and first cousin of James Napper Tandy, was married cir. 1760, to O'Brien Bellingham, Esq., third son of Alan Bellingham, of Castle Bellingham.

R. R. G. Crookshank, Major.*

---

# QUERIES.

### Letters Written to Archbishop King, 1680-1722.

Mr. John Hewetson (32 Cornwall Road, Bayswater, London, W.) would be glad for information leading to the discovery of three missing letters which formed part of the collection of the " Letters written to Archbishop King, between the years 1680 to 1722."

The first letter is dated 22nd March, 1698; the second, 31st July, 1700 ; and the third, 17th September, 1700.

These letters figure in the " Index " to them, but cannot now be found. They are supposed to be in Ireland, the possessor being an officer in the 2nd Life Guards.

---

### The Lister or Lyster Family.

The Rev. H. L. L. Denny (3 Lincoln Street, Sloane Square, London, S.W.) is preparing for publication a history of this family, and would be glad to get into communication with any persons who could supply him with information on its various branches.

---

* Died in July, 1911.

# BOOK NOTICE.

JACOBITE EXTRACTS FROM THE PARISH REGISTERS OF ST. GERMAIN-EN-LAYE. In two volumes. Price, £2 2s. By C. E. Lart.

The sojourn of the Stuarts at St. Germain-en-Laye lasted some thirty years, from their arrival in January, 1689, to the death of Queen Marie of Modena in 1719.

From 1688 onwards the Parochial Registers show an increasing number of baptisms, marriages, and deaths—roughly one-fifth of the total entries for the Parish. After the departure of the Chevalier de St. George in 1708, they tend to decrease until the death of Queen Mary in 1719. After that date a certain number occur to the end of the eighteenth century, chiefly of those adherents of the Stuarts who had settled down in the town and intermarried with the French population : the entries of deaths naturally increasing in proportion to marriages and baptisms.

A great number of Jacobites left St. Germains for Paris and other places, especially when the Royal Guard was disbanded after the death of James II, and the Irish Brigade was formed for the French Service. Many of them also returned to Great Britain.

It is proposed to publish these Registers, so far as they relate to Jacobite families, in two volumes—1689-1702, 1703-1720—each volume containing about 1,500 entries B.M.D.

The importance of these Registers is very great, since they will be found to fill up many gaps in English, Irish, and Scottish families, as well as supplying many hitherto unknown details.

The marriage entries are very full : the names of both parents of the married couple are given : whether widower or widow : and if so, the names of former husband or wife ; often details of former residence. The names of witnesses are also given, with their signatures, and the relationship to the contracting parties. Sometimes their parents are given, or the name of husband or wife of the witness, and their rank or profession.

The baptismal entries are very full, and the number of persons mentioned in each volume is not less than 7,000.

There are a large number of entries (B.M.D) relating to the families of Barry, Berwick, Bourke, Bulkeley, Butler, Callaghan, Clancarty, Coghlan, Connell, Conquest, Crane, Creagh, Dacre, D'Avia, Dillon, Douglas, Drummond, Fitz Gerald, Fitz James, Hamilton, Howard, Kennedy, Mac Carthy, Mac Mahon, Malony, Maitland, Middleton, Morphy, Nagle, Nugent, O'Brien, O'Donnell, O'Gara, O'Reilly, Plowden, Plunkett, Power, Roche, Sackville, Sheridan, Skelton, Stafford, Strickland, Talbot, Waldegrave, Walsh, besides many others : among which are found the names of Forster ;

Scrope, Wivell : with a host of lesser folk who flocked over in the train of the Stuarts.

An interesting feature in these Registers is the presence at St. Germains of notable Jacobites at particular dates, as attested by their signatures.

The work involved in transcribing has been very great, since it has been necessary to go through the Registers entry by entry. The difficulty of understanding the pronunciation of the names by the French scribe has led to strange versions of family names, especially those of Irish families. Thus Magrath becomes Megra ; Symes, Cime ; Reilly, Realy or Relle ; Murnahan, Murna. In many cases a Jacobite entry would have been passed over as a French one, but for the signature proving it to be a genuine Jacobite entry.

In other cases an entry has been held over until a later one of the same family has provided a clue. Thus Smath has turned out to be Smart, and not Smith ; and Flot, Foliott, and not Flood. Sometimes the clerk has despaired of a name, and has boldly transformed it into French—Welsh or Walsh more often than not becomes Vallois ; Bostock became Bostaque very soon, and remained so.

Some of the most important signatures have been reproduced, notably those of James II and his Queen ; James, Duc de Berwick ; James, Prince of Wales ; James, Grand Prior of England ; Sarsfield, Lucan, Middleton ; the Princess Louise of England ; Honora Burke, the Duc d'Albemarle, Sophia Bulkely, Clare, and others.

Some wills and papers will also be added in the appendix. These are among the residue of Stuart papers at Versailles which were not transferred to England. They are unimportant, though of interest, and consist mainly of accounts, procés, and wills. The most interesting is the deposition of Judith Wilkes, nurse to the Queen Mary, taken on her deathbed at St. Germains, testifying to the birth of the Chevalier de St. George at St. James's, in contradiction to the " warming-pan " story circulated by the Whigs.

Vol. I, B.M.D., 1689-1702, will be printed on hand-made paper, and issued for subscription at £1 1s. net.

Printed by Ponsonby & Gibbs, University Press, Dublin.

*Continuation of*

# Some

# Funeral Entries

## of

# Ireland.

*[From a Manuscript Volume in the British Museum.]*

**Francis Crispe** of Lissmayne in the County of Killkenny (669)
Gent., 2ᵈ Son of Joseph Crispe of Parkesgrove in the Said
County Gent. descendᵈ of the House of Cobrutt in the County
of Oxford.

The said Francis married Frances Datʳ of John Dryland
of Nye in the County of Kent in England Gent. by whom
he had issue 9 Children viz. William, Elizabeth, Frances,
Margaret, Ellen, Ann and Mary Crispe.

The 1ˢᵗ mentioned Francis died at Lissmayne aforsaid the
17ᵗʰ of October 1638 and was Interrᵈ in our Ladies Church in
the Citty of Killkenny.

The truith of the prmssˢ is testᵈ by Subscriptⁿ of Frances Page 326
Relict and Executrix of the Defnᵗ the 13ᵗʰ of Novemʳ 16 . .

FRANCES CRISPE.

**James** mᶜᶜ Willᵐ **o' Farell** of Ballymaghane in the (670)
County of Longford Gent. Son of William o' Farell of
the Sᵈ James died          The said James maried
the Datʳ of          Dillon of Baskenaugh in the
County of West Meath Gent. by whom he had 2 Sons and
1 Datʳ viz. Hobert eldest Son mar'd to          datʳ of
o' Molloy of          ; 2ᵈ Son not marᵈ; Margaret marᵈ to
Rossa o' Fearroll of Faslewart in the County of Longford
Gent. The Said James 2ˡʸ marᵈ Annable Datʳ of Hugh
ô Kelly of Ballagh in the County Roscomon Gent. by whom
he had issue 4 Datʳˢ / viz. Jane eldᵗ Dat.          Page 327.

The 1ˢᵗ mentioned James died at Ballymahane aforsaid
about the 20ᵗʰ of Decemʳ 1639 and was interr'd in the parish
Church of Sruhell about the 23ᵈ of the same Month. The
truith of the premssˢ is testᵈ by subscripⁿ of the Said Annable
who returned this Certificate into my Office to be there
recorded.

Taken by me Thomas Preston Esqʳ Ulster King of Arms
the 4ᵗʰ of March 1639.

**The Rt Honble Ellinor** Viscountess Dillon of Castillo (671)
Gallene Datʳ of William Tuite of Tuitestowne in the County This is
of West Meath Esqʳ. She was married to Theobald the 1ˢᵗ entd. page
Viscᵗ Dillon of Castillo-gallane by whom She had issue 7 Sons 265.
and 10 Datʳˢ; viz Sʳ Christophʳ Dillon eldᵗ Son and Heir
mar'd to the Lady Jane Dillon datʳ of the Rᵗ Honᵇˡe James
Earle of Roscommon, wᶜʰ Sʳ Christopʳ Died / in the Life Page 328.
time of his Father leaving issue Luke eldest Son who was
marᵈ to the Lady Mary datʳ of Randall 1ˢᵗ Earle of Antrim
by whom he had issue Theobald Viscᵗ Dillon who Died an
Infant. Thomas 2ᵈ Son of the said Sʳ Christopʳ by the Death

15 *

of the last ment<sup>d</sup> Theobald without issue now Lo<sup>d</sup> Visc<sup>t</sup> Dillon of Castillo-gallane and mar<sup>d</sup> to Frances dat<sup>r</sup> of S<sup>r</sup> Rich<sup>d</sup> White Kn<sup>t</sup>; Theobald 3<sup>d</sup> Son of the Said Christopper; James 4<sup>th</sup> both as yet not mar<sup>d</sup>; Charles 5<sup>th</sup>; Francis 6<sup>th</sup>; and Christop. 7<sup>th</sup> died Infants. Ellenor eld<sup>t</sup> and Mary 2<sup>d</sup> Dat<sup>r</sup> of the Said S<sup>r</sup> Christop<sup>r</sup> both died being not mar<sup>d</sup>. Jane 3<sup>d</sup> Dat<sup>r</sup> mar<sup>d</sup> to John Maddin of Longford in Com Gallway Esq<sup>r</sup>; Elizabeth 4<sup>th</sup> and Margarett 5<sup>th</sup> both as yet not mar<sup>d</sup>

**Page 329.**  S<sup>r</sup> Lucas Dillon 2<sup>d</sup> Son of the S<sup>d</sup> Theobald first Visc<sup>t</sup> Dillon and of the S<sup>d</sup> Visc<sup>ss</sup> Ellenor, mar<sup>d</sup> to Jane Dat<sup>r</sup> of John Moore of Bryess in the County of Mayo Esq; William Dillon 3<sup>d</sup> Son of the S<sup>d</sup> Theobald and Ellenor y<sup>e</sup> Visc<sup>ss</sup> mar<sup>d</sup> to Margery dat<sup>r</sup> of James Magawly of Ballyloghloe / in Com West Meath Esq<sup>r</sup>; Thomas 4<sup>th</sup> Son of the Said Theo<sup>d</sup> & Visc<sup>ss</sup> Ellenor mar<sup>d</sup> to Katherin dat<sup>r</sup> of Morish Fitz Gerald of Leccagh in the County of Killdare Esq<sup>r</sup>; Edward 5<sup>th</sup> Son of the Said Theob<sup>d</sup> & Visc<sup>ss</sup> as yet not mar<sup>d</sup>; S<sup>r</sup> James Dillon 6<sup>th</sup> Son was mar<sup>d</sup> to Elizabeth Dat<sup>r</sup> of Thomas Plunkett of Rathmore in the County of Meath Esq<sup>r</sup> w<sup>ch</sup> Elizabeth Died without issue; George, 7<sup>th</sup> Son of the Said Theob<sup>d</sup> as yett not mar<sup>d</sup>. Margarett eld<sup>t</sup> dat<sup>r</sup> of the S<sup>d</sup> Theobald and Visc<sup>ss</sup> Ellenor mar<sup>d</sup> to Robert Dillon of Connorstowne in the County of West Meath Esq<sup>r</sup>; Mary 2<sup>d</sup> dat<sup>r</sup> mar<sup>d</sup> to Garrett Petitt of Irishtowne in the S<sup>d</sup> County of West Meath Esq<sup>r</sup>; Elizabeth 3<sup>d</sup> Dat<sup>r</sup> mar<sup>d</sup> to Thomas Fitz Gerald of Criveagh in Com. Longford Esq<sup>r</sup>; Jennett 4<sup>th</sup> Dat<sup>r</sup> mar<sup>d</sup> to Hugh ô Connor of Castlereogh in the County of Roscomon Esq<sup>r</sup>; Ann 5th mar<sup>d</sup> to John Lo<sup>d</sup> Visc<sup>t</sup> Taaff of Correne and Baron of Ballymote; Katherin 6<sup>th</sup> da<sup>r</sup> mar<sup>d</sup> to S<sup>r</sup> Ullick Bourke of Glinske in the

**Page 330.**  S<sup>d</sup> Com Roscomon Knt and Baronett; Ellenor 7<sup>th</sup>, Cicely 8<sup>th</sup>, both not mar<sup>d</sup>, Bridget 9<sup>th</sup>, and Barbara 10<sup>th</sup>, both died being not mar<sup>d</sup>.

The first mention<sup>d</sup> Visc<sup>ss</sup> died at Killynure in Com West Meath the 8<sup>th</sup> of Apll 1638 and was Interr'd in S<sup>t</sup> Francis Abby in Athlone.

The truth of the premss<sup>s</sup> is test<sup>d</sup> by Subscript<sup>n</sup> of S<sup>r</sup> James Dillon Knt 6<sup>th</sup> Son of the S<sup>d</sup> Theobald, who return'd this Certificate into my Office to be there record<sup>d</sup>  Taken by me Thomas Preston, Esq<sup>r</sup>, Ulster King of Armes, the 10th of July 1638.

(672) (Arms.)  **Honor dat<sup>r</sup> and one of the Coheirs of S<sup>r</sup> John Dowdall** of Kilfeny in the County of Limerick Kn<sup>t</sup>, who was Son of S<sup>r</sup> John Dowdall Kn<sup>t</sup>, who was Son of S<sup>r</sup> William Dowdall Kn<sup>t</sup>. She was mar<sup>d</sup> to Lawrence Dowdall Son and Heir of Edward Dowdall of Mountown Esq<sup>r</sup>, Regest<sup>r</sup> of the

High Court of Chancery of Ireland, by whom She had issue /
Dat$^r$ viz. Elizabeth. The S$^d$ Honor died the 2$^d$ of Octob$^r$ 1638
and was Inter$^d$ in the Parish Church of Mountown als
Monckstowne the 5$^{th}$ of y$^e$ same Month. The truth of the
premss$^s$ is tes$^d$ by Edward Dowdall afores$^d$. Taken by me
Albon Leveret, Athlone to be record$^d$ in the King of Arms
office this 12$^{th}$ of Nouember 1638.

E. Dowdall.

**Malby Brabazon** of Ballynesloe in the County of Page 331.
Roscommon Esq$^r$, eld$^t$ Son of Cap$^t$ Anthony Brabazon and of (673)
Ursula his Wife, Dater of Nicholas Malby of Roscommon
aforesaid Kn$^t$, which Cap$^t$ Anthony was 2$^d$ Brother of William
Baron of Ardee. The 1$^{st}$ ment$^d$ Malby Brabzon was mar$^d$ to
Sarah dat$^r$ of Thomas Bourke of Tulaeyry in the County of
Gallway and by her had issue 1 Son and 3 Da$^{rs}$, Anthony as
yet not mar$^d$ ; Ursula eld$^t$ Dater mard to Bernard Talbott of
Rathdowne in the County of Wicklow Gent. ; Sarah 2$^d$ Dat$^r$,
and Dorothy 3$^d$, both as yett not mar$^d$. The 1$^{st}$ ment$^d$ Malby
died at Ballinasloe afors$^d$ the 20th Day of May last past and
is to be Inter'd in the Parish Church of _____ in the
Said County of Roscommon upon the _____ of June
1637.
To be test$^d$ by Anthony only Son and Heir.

**James Stack** of Callowhill in the County of Farmanagh, (674)
Clarke and Parson of Iniskeane in the Said County. The
said / James mar$^d$ Martha dat$^r$ of Edward Hatton, Archdeacon Page 332.
of Ardagh, and by her had issue 4 Sons and 3 Dat$^s$ viz.
Edward eld$^t$ Son mar$^d$ to
James 2$^d$, Willm 3$^d$, George 4$^{th}$ Son. Judith eld$^t$ Dat$^r$
mar$^d$ to Thomas Suggden of Lissymeane in the County of
Cavan Gent. ; Susan 2$^d$ Dat$^r$, and Margarett 3$^d$ Dat$^r$, both as
yet not mar$^d$. The 1$^{st}$ mentioned James died at Dublin in
May 1634 and was inter'd in St Katherin's Church Dublin.
The truith hereof is test$^d$ by Patrick Brien this 24$^{th}$ of Aug$^t$
1637.

Patrick Brene.

**Thomas Swords als Croly** of Drogheda Alderman Son (675)
and Heir of Edmond Swords of the same Merchant, died at
Drogheda aforsaid the 27th of July 1636 and was Inter$^d$ in
the Parish Church of S$^t$ Peters in the Said Towne. The
Def$^t$ mar$^d$ Mary dat$^r$ of George Pippard of Drogheda and
Widdow of _____ White of the Said Towne / Merch$^t$ and Page 333.
Alderm$^n$ by whom He had issue 12 Children viz Anthony,

Thomas, Edmond, Ann, and Katherin, all the rest of the S^d 12 Died young. The truith of the P̃remss^s is test^d by the Subscript^n of the Said Mary relict and administratrix of the Def^t who return'd this Certif^t to be record^d in the Office of Ulster King of Armes. Taken this 21^st of Septem^r 1636.

MARY PIPARD.

(676) Richad Lutterell of Tancardstown, Son and Heir of Robt, 2^d Son of S^r Thomas Lutterell of Lutterellstowne in the County of Dublin, Kn^t, died at Tancardstowne afors^d the of October 1633 and was Inter^d in the Parish of Donaghpatrick in the County of Meath ; he mar^d Ann dat^r of Robert Cussake of Cussingstowne in the S^d County, by whom He had issue 4 Children viz. 2 Sons and 2* Daters viz. Oliver eld^t who mar^d Margery dat^r of Tibbott Wealsh of Killincorige in the County of Wicklow Gent by whom he hath issue 8 Children viz 5 Sons and 3 Dat^rs, Robert, John, James, / Michaell, and Bartholomew, Margarett, Mary, and Frances. The truith of the premss^s is test^d p̃ Subscript^n of Oliver Lutterell who returned this Certif^t to be recorded in the Office of Ulster King of Armes. Taken by me Thomas Preston Esq^r, Ulster King of Armes ye 3^d of Novem^r 1635.

*James 2nd Son unmar. Jenn eldest daugh. mar^d. Rolan Plunkett of Rochelstoune in y^e Com. Meaith, Mary 2^d Dau. mar^d. to George Bath of Edixstowne in y^e s^d. County Gentt.

Page 334.

OL : LUTTERELL.

(677) Stephen Leonard of the Citty of Waterford Gent 2^d Son but by the Death of his eld^r Broth^r Heir of Alexander Leonard Alderm^n of the same.

The S^d Stephen mard Cicely dat^r of James Levett of the Citty afors^d, by whom he hath 4 Sons and 3 Dat^rs, viz. Alexander eld^t Son, John 2^d, James 3^d, and Alexander 4^th, died an Infant and the rest as yett not mar^d ; Anstace eld^t Dat^r, Mary 2^d, Ellen 3^d, all young and not mar^d. The first ment^d Stephen died in the S^d Citty the 14^th of A      1638 and was interr^d in Our Ladies Chappell the 16^th of the same Month. The truith of the premss^s is test^d by Subscript^n of John Lee Broth^r-in-Law / of the Def^t, who return'd this Certif^t into my office to be there recorded. Taken by me Thomas Preston Esq^r, Ulster King of Armes, the 4th of Decem^r 1638.

Page 335.

JOHN LEE.

(678) (Arms.) Elizabeth dat^r of Robert Haris of y^e Derie, High Sheriff of the County of Donnegall or Callran Esq^r died the 4th of July and was buried in the Church of S^t Warbroughs the 7^th of the same Month 1635. She was mar^d to William

Scott Search$^e$ of His Ma$\tilde{t}$ies port of Dublin Esq$^r$ by whom He had issue William, Henry Robert and Edward. The truith of the premss$^s$ is test$^d$ by Subscript$^n$ of the S$^d$ William Scott Serch$^e$. Taken by me Albon Leveret Athlone Officer of Armes to be recorded in the Office of the King of Armes of Ireland.

WILLM SCOTT.

**Robert O'Ferrall** of the Bawne in the County of Long- (679) ford Esq$^e$ Died the 10$^{th}$ of May 1634 and was buried in the Parish Church of Mydowe in the Said Co$\tilde{m}$. He mar$^d$ first Page 336. Margery dat$^r$ of / Robert Nangle of Balesax in the County of Killdare Esq$^e$ and by her had 1 Son, viz. Richard o'Ferrall Son and Heir ; and 6 Dat$^{rs}$, Ellenor, Elizabeth, Kat$^n$, Marg$^t$, Margery, and Joan. He 2$^{ly}$ mary'd Ônor dat$^r$ of Gerald Fitz Gerald of Gleselly, Esq$^e$ and by her had 1 dat$^r$ viz. Ann. The Truith of the premss$^s$ is test$^d$ by the Subscript$^n$ of Roger Nangle who returned this Certif$^t$ to be record$^d$ in the Office of Ulster King of Armes. The 10$^{th}$ of Novem$^r$ 1635.

ROGER NANGLE.

**Thomas Aylmer** of Lyons in the County of Killdare (680) Esq$^e$, eld$^t$ Son and Heir of Bartholomew Aylmer of the same Esq$^e$, eld$^t$ Son and Heir of Thomas Aylmer of the same Esq$^e$ Chief of that name in the Kingdome of Ireland. The 1$^{st}$ ment$^d$ Thomas mar$^d$ Mabell dat$^r$ of S$^r$ Patrick Barnwall of Turvye, Kn$^t$, by whom he had no issue. The said Thomas died the 3$^d$ of Novem$^r$ 1639 and was Inter$^d$ in the Parish Church of Lyons afors$^d$. The truith of y$^e$ premss$^s$ is test$^d$ by Subscript$^n$ of George Aylmer Esq$^e$, next Brother and Heir of the Defun$^t$ who return'd this Certif$^t$ to be record$^d$ in the Office of Ulster King of Armes the 5$^{th}$ of Decem$^r$ 1639.

GEORGE AYLMER.

**Thomas Mayne** of the Citty of Waterford Sheriff, eld$^t$ Page 337. Son of Henry Mayne of the same Merchant, died in May 1634 (681) and was inter'd in St. Francis Abby in the said Citty. He (Arms.) mar$^d$ An dat$^r$ of Thomas Nele of the said Citty by whom he left issue 1 Son and 3 Dat$^{rs}$ viz. Henry eld$^t$ Son of the Def$^t$ ; Ellen eld$^t$ Dat$^r$ mar$^d$ to Geratt Lincolne of the same Citty ; Katherin married to Laurence Denn ; and Beale as yett not mar$^d$. The truith of the premss$^s$ is test$^d$ by Subscript$^n$ of Ann Mayne Relict of the Said Thomas, who returned this Certificate into the Office of Ulst$^r$ King of Armes, taken the 13$^{th}$ of June 1636.

Sig$\tilde{n}$a ANN MAYNE.

(682)　　　　**Edmond Kearny** of Cashell in the County of Tipperary
Esq⁰ Son of　　　　　　　　The said Edmond mar^d
Katherin dat^r of Edmond Boyton of the same, Burgess, by
whom he had issue 6 Sons and 4 Dat^rs viz. William eld^t Son
maryed to Ellice dat^r of George Boyton of Cashell Burgess;
Thomas 2^d Son, Nicholas 3^d, Patrick 4^th, Ignatius 5^th, and
James 6^th; Onora eldest Dat^r maryed to Nicholas Conway of
Cashell Merchant; Ellice 2^d mar^d to Richard Conway of the
Page 338.　Same Merchant; Annstace 3^d, and Ann 4^th Dat^r. The Said
Edmond died the 12^th of Octob^r 1633, and was Inter^d in the
Cathedrall Church of S^t Patricks at Cashell the 15^th of the
same Month. The truith of the premss^s is test^d by Sub-
script^n of the S^d William eld^t Son of the Def^t who returned
this Certif^t into my Office to be there recorded. Taken by me
Thomas Preston Esq⁰ Ulster King of Armes the 29^th of July
1635.

　　　　　　　　　　　　　　　　WILLM. KEARNEY.

(683)　　　　**John Richardson** of Levallieglish als Lowgall in the
County of Ardmagh, Clarke, and Justic of Peace in the S^d
Com̃., 2^d Son of John Richardson of Warmington in the
County of Warwick in England Gent. He mar^d Ellenor
Barnett, eld^t Dat^r of William Barnett of Harwich in England
Gent; he had by her 8 Children viz. 4 Sons John eld^t, Robert
2^d died, Samuell 3^d,　　　　　4^th; and 4 Dat^rs viz. Ellizabeth
eld^t, Ann 2^d, Ellenor 3^d, Mary 4^th, all living. He died the
25^th day of September Anno dom 1634 and was Interr'd in
the Parish Church of Evallieglish afors^d all w^ch is test^d by
Ellenor Richardson Widdow, the 3^d of Decem^r Anno Dom̃.
1635.

　　　　　　　　　　　　Her
　　　　　ELLENOR　E R　RICHARDSON.
　　　　　　　　　　　　Mark.

　　Witness
　　HENRY BRAME.

Page 339.　　　**Christopher Pippart** of Drogheda Merchant 2^d Son of
(684)　　　George Pippart of the same Alderm^n Died at Drogheda the
6^th of March 1635 and was Inter'd in S^t Peter's Church in
the Said Towne　The Defunct mar^d first
dat^r of Christop^r Fleming of the Newry Merchant, by who he
had issue 2 Sons and 2 Dat^rs viz. Thomas and Edward both
died young, Margery and Mary. The Def^t 2^ly mar'd Margarett
dat^r of Thomas Brady of Drogheda Gent. by whom he had
4 Sons and 1 Dat^r viz. George and Richard both died young,
Thomas and Ignatius now Living; Ismay the only Dat^r now

living. The truith of the premss$^s$ is test$^d$ by subscript$^n$ of
Margarett Relict of the Defunct who returned this Certif$^t$ to
be record$^d$ in the Office of Ulster King of Armes the 20th of
1636.

**Henry Gould** 2 Son of Adam Gould of the Citty of (685)
Corke Alderm$^n$ died at Corke afors$^d$ in May 1634 and was
Inter'd in Christ Church in the S$^d$ Citty. He mar$^d$ first
Ellen dat$^r$ of Morice Roch in the S$^d$ Citty Alderm$^n$, by whom
he had 7 Children viz. 2 Sons and 5 / Dat$^{rs}$ viz James eld$^t$ Son Page 340.
who mar$^d$ the Dat$^r$ of Thomas Alderman
by whom he had issue one Son viz Henry ; John 2$^d$ Son of
the Def$^t$ mary$^d$ to Ellenor dat$^r$ of Henry Verdon of the S$^d$
Citty Gent. ; Ellen eld$^t$ Dat$^r$ mar$^d$ to John Gallway of the S$^d$
Citty Gent. ; Joan y$^e$ 2$^d$ mar$^d$ to Edmond Gould of the Said
Citty Gent. ; Katherin 3$^d$ mar$^d$ to David Meagh of the Said
Citty ; 4$^{th}$ as yett not mar$^d$, Jennet youngest not
mar'd. The truith of the premss$^s$ is test$^d$ by Subscript$^n$ of
Adam Gould of the Said Citty Sheriff and Cozen Germon of
the Def$^t$, who returned this Certif$^t$ into my Office to be
record$^d$. The s$^d$ Henry was 2$^{ly}$ mar$^d$ to Ellen dat$^r$ of John
Verdon of the S$^d$ Citty Gent. by whom he had 1 Son and
2 Dat$^{rs}$ viz. Francis, Elliph and Alson. The truith of the
premss$^s$ is test$^d$ by Subscript$^n$ of Adam Gould afors$^d$ who
returd this Certif$^t$ into the Office of Ulster King of Armes,
taken the 12 of Novem$^r$ 1635.

ADAM GOULD.

**William Talbott** of Wiexford, Mayor, 2$^d$ Son of Patrick (686)
Talbott of the same, Mayor, died at Wiexford Novemb$^r$ 1634
and was Inter'd in S$^t$ Marys Church in Wiexford. The def$^t$
mar$^d$ Katherin dat$^r$ of Walter / Wadding of the same Mer- Page 341.
chant, by whom he had 2 Sons and 2 Dat$^{rs}$ viz. John eld$^t$ son,
Patricke, Mary eld$^t$ dat$^r$ mar$^d$ to Patrick Lumbart of the same
mar$^d$ to James Chivers of Dublin Merch$^t$
He 2$^{ly}$ mard Joane Dat$^r$ of Patrick Sinotte of Ballycrom in
the County of Waxford Gent., Widdow of Edward Eustace,
Gent., by whom He had issue Sons viz. James mar'd to
; Walter; Mary mar'd to James Codd
of Clogheast in the County of Waxford Gent ; Martha and
Ellenor. The truith of the premss$^s$ is test$^d$ by Subscript$^n$ of
Nicholas Sinotte, Broth$^r$ of the Said Joan, who return'd this
Certificate to be record'd in the office of Ulster King of
Armes June the 11$^{th}$ 1636.

NICHOLAS SYNNOTTE.

(687)   Willm Butler in the County of Tipp^y, Gent.,        son
and Heir of John Butler of the                    He died in
Febru^e 1633 and was Inter'd in the Abby of Clonmell in the
S^d Com̃. He mar^d Ellin dat^r of Coĺĺ. m^cc Shyne in the said
County Gent. by whom He had 6 Sons and 5 Dat^rs viz.
Richard eld^t Son who mar^d 1^st Margarett Dat^r of Pierce Butler
Page 342. of Ballyroutty in the said Com̃. and 2^ly Ellen dat^r of Theobald
Butler Lo^d Baron of / Cary in Com̃. Tipperar^e ; James 2^d Son
mar^d 1^st Ellin dat^r of Edmond Tobine of Kilneganuagh in the
S^d Com̃ and 2^ly Ellis ; Walter 3^d mar^d Joan Dat^r of John
English of Balleroch in Com̃. Tipp^y ; Pierce 4^th who mar^d
Joan dat^r of Walter Butler of the same Com̃., he 2^ly mar^d
Ellis dat^r of James Finnell of the same County ; Edmond 5^th
who mar^d Margarett Dat^r of m^cc Laffan in the Said County ;
Theobald 6^th a Command^e of a Regiment of Souldiers in
Garmany, who mar^d Ellenor Dat^r of m^cc Rockett in the
County of Waterford ; Edward 7^th who mar^d Margaret dat^r of
Edmond Tobine of the S^d Com̃.; Ellis eld^t Dat^r mar^d to
Richard          ; Katherin 2^d, Ellis 3^d, Ellan, Joan died
young, Katherin mar^d to Jeffry Power of Fedan in Com̃
Waterford, Ellan y^e 3^d mar^d to James Fitz Gerald in the
Waterford, Joan 4^th mar^d to Thomas Tobine of the Bristelagh
in Com̃ Tipp^y, Ellis 1^st mar^d to John Manachan 2^ly to Connor
ô Mulryan.

(688)    John m^cc Gibbon Bourk of Claddagh in the County
of Mayo, Gent., 3^d Son of Geffry m^cc Gibbon Bourk of the
Same Gent, - - eld^t Son of Janack m^cc Gibbon Bourk of the
same Gent. descended of y^e house of
Page 343. The 1^st ment^d John mar^d Grany dat^r of William ^mcc Moyler
m^cc Gibbon Bourk of Coshen Gent. and Relict of Redmond
Jonyn of Carrig Ichoully in the same County Gent., by which
Redmond she had 2 Dat^rs, and by ^Wch Grany the first men-
tion'd John had issue 2 Sons and 2 Dat^rs viz. Richard eld^t
and Hubert 2^d neith^r of y^em being mard. . . . . . . .
dat^r of the s^d John mar^d to William oge m^cc Gibbon Bourk of
Carrigginedy in the S^d Com̃ Mayo Gent; S . . . . . .
2^d dat^r not yett mard. The S^d John died at Killroe in Com̃
Mayo about the 1^st of          1633 and was inter'd in the
Parish Church of Aghagowre in the Said County of Mayo
The truith of the premss^s is test^d by subscript^n of the Said
William oge m^cc Gibbon Bourk Son-in-law of the Defunct
who return'd this certif^t into my Office to be there recorded.
Taken by me Thomas Preston Esq^e Ulster King of Armes
May y^e 17^th 1638.

                              WILLM GIBBON.

**Jhosua Lancaster** of the Grange in Com̃ Tipperary Page 344. Esq<sup>e</sup> died at the Grange in October 1634 He was 2<sup>d</sup> Son of (689) the Rev<sup>d</sup> Father in God Lo<sup>d</sup> Bpp of Waterford and Lismore He mar'd Mary dat<sup>r</sup> of Gilbert Waters of Cullin in the S<sup>d</sup> Com̃ of Cross Tipperary by whom He had issue one Dat<sup>r</sup> viz. Elizabeth The truith of the premss<sup>s</sup> is test<sup>d</sup> by subscript<sup>n</sup> of William Waters. Taken Septem<sup>r</sup> y<sup>e</sup> 8<sup>th</sup> 1635.

WILL : WATERS.

**Mary dat<sup>r</sup> of Patrick Hogan** of Lissnemony in the (690) County of Clare Esq<sup>e</sup> was mar'd to John Fanynge of Limrick Merchant Son of
The said Mary died (11<sup>th</sup> of Decem<sup>r</sup> Anno Dom̃. 1638) Inter'd in the Parish Church of                       in Limirick.
The truith of the premss<sup>s</sup> is test<sup>d</sup> by Subscript<sup>n</sup> of the Said Page 345. John / Fanynge Husband of the Said Mary who hath returned this Certiff<sup>t</sup> into my Office to be there recorded. Taken by me Thomas Preston Esq<sup>e</sup> Ulster King of Armes, the 21<sup>st</sup> of May Anno Dom̃. 1639.

JO : FANYNG.

**S<sup>r</sup> Nicholas Mordant** of Carrick in y<sup>e</sup> County of Clare, (691) Kt, died the    —    of August 1623 ; he had to wife Sarah (Arms.) daughter of William Stockdalle of Greenhamerton in Yorkshire, by whom he had Issue Nicholas.— Taken by Athlone.

**Pierce Butler** of Nodstowne in y<sup>e</sup> County of Tipparary (692) Esq<sup>e</sup> died the 21 of february 1626 ; he had to Wife Elan (Arms.) Daughter of Thomas Pursell Barron of Loughmore, and had Issue James who haith to wife Elanor Second Daughter of S<sup>r</sup> John Fitz Gerald of Dromana in y<sup>e</sup> County of Waterford Kt ; Richard, Elan, Joan, Elanor, and Margarett. He was buried in y<sup>e</sup> Abby of Holie Crosse    —    Taken by Athlone

(The following is on a page inserted in the MS. between folios 345 and 346.)

**Katherin, daughter of Robert Drury** of Laughlin (693) in the County of Catherlogh Esq<sup>e</sup>, and wife of S<sup>r</sup> John King, K<sup>nt</sup>, Muster = Master Gen<sup>ll</sup>, and of y<sup>e</sup> privy Councill, deceased y<sup>e</sup> 14<sup>th</sup> of December 1617. She left Issue by the s<sup>d</sup> Sir John as you will find in y<sup>e</sup> Certificate underneath.

**The R<sup>t</sup> Hon<sup>ble</sup> S<sup>r</sup> John King** of Abby-Boyle in the County of Roscomon, K<sup>nt</sup>, Muster-Master of Ireland, did marry Katherin daughter of Robert Drury of Laughlin in the County of Catherlogh, Esq<sup>r</sup>, by whom he had issue six sons and three

Daughters, viz<sup>t</sup>, Sir Robert King son and heyre apparent hath to wife Frances daughter of y<sup>e</sup> late R<sup>t</sup> Hon<sup>ble</sup> S<sup>r</sup> Henry ffolliott K<sup>nt</sup>, Lord ffolliott Baron of Ballyshannon ; John King Esq<sup>r</sup> 2<sup>d</sup> son and sometime Clarke of his Matyes Hanaper-Office, did marry Margarett daughter of ffrancis Edgeworth Esq<sup>r</sup> Clarke likewise of y<sup>e</sup> Hanaper-Office sometime ; Roger King 3<sup>d</sup> son, Edward King 4<sup>th</sup> son, Henry King 5<sup>th</sup> son, and Adam King 6<sup>th</sup> son ; Mary marryed to y<sup>e</sup> R<sup>t</sup> Hon<sup>ble</sup> S<sup>r</sup> Will<sup>m</sup> Caulfield K<sup>nt</sup>, Lord Caulfield Baron of Charlemount, and sometime Master of y<sup>e</sup> Ordnance and one of the Privy Councill of Ireland ; Margarett marryed to Sir Gerrard Lowther K<sup>nt</sup> Lord Chiefe Justice of his Matyes Court of Comon Pleas, and one of the Privy Councill ; Dorothy was marryed to Arthur Moore Esq<sup>r</sup> 3<sup>d</sup> son of S<sup>r</sup> Garrett Moore K<sup>nt</sup> Baron of Mellifont and Viscount Moore of Drogheda.

The above said Sir John King departed this mortall life y<sup>e</sup> 4<sup>th</sup> day of January 1636, and was interr'd in the Church of Abby-Boyle w<sup>th</sup> funerall Rites according to his degree y<sup>e</sup> 30th of March 1637. The truth of y<sup>e</sup> premises is testifyed by y<sup>e</sup> Subscription of S<sup>r</sup> Robert King of Abby Boyle afores<sup>d</sup> K<sup>nt</sup>. Taken by me Albone Leveret Athlone-Officer at Arms, to be recorded in y<sup>e</sup> Office of y<sup>e</sup> King of Arms.

All w<sup>ch</sup> I find recorded in y<sup>e</sup> Office of Ulster King of Arms of all Ireland, As wittnesse my name and title this 25<sup>th</sup> day of September 1697.

RICHARD CARNEY Ulster King of Armes of all Ireland.

a true Coppy.

Page 346. (694) **Robert Drury** of Callow in y<sup>e</sup> County of Roscomon Esq<sup>r</sup> was the onely son of Thomas Drury of Laughlin in the County of Catherlogh Esq<sup>r</sup> and of Margarett de la Freigne daughter of Robert de la Freigne, and of Katherin Butler, of Ballyready in the County of Kilkenny ; wich Thomas was the onely son of Robert Drury of Laughlin afores<sup>d</sup> Esq<sup>r</sup> and of Elizabeth Carew, sister of S<sup>r</sup> Peter Carew K<sup>t</sup> call'd Baron of Idrone (descended with other Estates to y<sup>e</sup> Carew's his ancestors from the Heyres generall of Raymond le Grosse, and Robert Fitz Stephen two of the first Conquerors of Ireland) which Robert Drury was 2<sup>d</sup> son of Edmond Drury of Horton in Com : Bucks, and of Jeane, daughter of Thomas Trenchard of Lichett in Dorsett-shire Esq<sup>r</sup> and sister to Henry Trenchard ; w<sup>ch</sup> Edmond was 4<sup>th</sup> son of S<sup>r</sup> Robert Drury of Hedgerley in Com Bucks K<sup>t</sup> and Brother of S<sup>r</sup> William Drury of Weston in Com Oxōn K<sup>t</sup> Lord President of Munster in Anno 1576 and

Lord Dep^{ty} of Ireland in Anno 1578 ; which S^r Robert was 2^d son of S^r Robert Drury of Hawsted in Com̃ Suffolk K^t, a Privy Counsellor to King Henry y^e 7^{th} and King Henry y^e 8^{th} and Brother to S^r William Drury of Hawsted affors^d K^t a Privy Counsellor to Qeen Mary. The first mentioned Robert Drury took to wife Margarett, daughter of Thomas Lloyd and Honor Price of Clòone in the County Leitrim, but first of Flint- and Denby-Shires in Wales, by whom he had issue 5 sons and 5 daughters (viz^t) Robert, eldest son who dyed young ; John 2^d son and heyre now of Hawsted als Callaw afores^d ; who took to wife, Grace, daughter of James Walcope, and of Margarett Maxwell of Dromanelis, and Finebroge in y^e County Downe, and had Issue: 4 sons and 4 daughters (viz.) John, William ; Valeria, Henrietta, Jeane, and Mary, but all dyed young, William 3^d son died y^e 17^{th} of Aprill 1680.

L^t Edward Drury 4^{th} son now of Kingsland in y^e County Roscomon who took to wife Elizabeth daughter of S^r Francis Gore K^t and of Ann Parks of Sligoe and hath issue 2 sons and 6 daughters (viz.) John eldest son, now liveing, Robert 2^d son dyed young, Margarett, eldest daughter, Ann 2^d, Jeane 3^d, Elizabeth 4^{th}, Frances 5 and . . . . 6^{th} Daughter. Major Robert Drury 5^{th} son now liveing unmarryed, Katherin, eldest daughter died young, Elizabeth 2^d died young, Margarett, 3^d daughter marryed to John Forster of Tullaghan in the County of Monoghan Clke, by whom she had severall children who dyed young, and she deceased y^e 25^{th} of December 1679, Jeane, 4^{th} daughter dyed . . . August 1684 unmarryed, Frances 5^{th} daughter marryed to Michaell Mosse of Bandon Clke (nephew to the R^t Reverand Richard Boyle Bishopp of Laughlin and Fernes, and Roger Boyle Bishopp of Downe and Conōr, and afterwards of Clogher) by whom Shee left one daughter Jeane Mosse, now liveing unmarryed, and dyed . . . . . 1690. The aboue said Robert Drury first named departed this Mortall life in the 63 yeare of his age on y^e 13^{th} of January 1673 and the said Margarett, his wife in the 57 yeare of her age likwise deceased on y^e 3^d of May 1677. Both were buryed with funerall Rites according to their degrees, and lye interred under one Tombstone in the Chancell (railed in, and Shingled for them and their family's Page 347. / Burying-place, before the late Troubles, but in that disorderly Time broke down) in the Abby of Cloonshanvoyle in the County of Roscomon. The truth of the premisses is Testified by the Subscription of y^e said John Drury Esq^r 2^d son and heyre of y^e said Robert and Margarett, his honored Father and Mother, Entred the 8^{th} of September 1712.

J. Drury.

Heton
Midhopp
(695)
(Arms).

DEUS
FORTI-
TUDO
MEA

(696)
(Arms.)
Toole.

Mrs           Daughter of Toole als Tooley  .  .
She was buried at St James Church Dublin With Scocheons
octr the 17th 1700.

(697)
(Arms.)
Shouldrum

Dame Elir Shouldrom of Norfolk, Shee was Buried
In the parish Church of Sat Bridgett's Dublinn with Scocheons
July the 12th 1703
This Coat is Impaled on the grave Stone with a Lyon
Rampant, Sinister Side [ ___crest___ ] Crest of Shouldrem.

(698)
(Arms.)
Marsh :
Dodwell.

Mrs Dodwell  Shee was married to the Reverend Jeremy
Marsh.  Shee died in England And was Intered In the Church
of Athlone with Scocheons  She was Daughter to Henry
Dodwell Esqr October the 9th 1703.

Page 348.
(Arms.)
Barring-
ton :
Wheeler.
(699)

Crest a falcon Standing on a Ducal Coronet pp Wheeler.

Mrs Wheeler  She was married To Coll; Barrington
and was Interred with Scocheons Att St Audeons Church
october the 9th 1703.

(700)
(Arms.)
Maud.

Dame nancy Maud Daughter of Coll: Maud of
Killkenny  She Dyed near St Andrews Church Dublin and
was buried In Killkenny with Scocheons october the 30th
1704.

(701)
(Arms.)
Price.

Mrs Francies Price Daughter of John Price Esqr Constable of the Castle of Dublin and Vice Treasurer of Ireland
She was Interred In Christ Church Dublin October the 26th
1704 with Scocheons.

(702)
(Arms.)
Blundell :
Ingolsby.

Dame Anne Blundell was Intered with Scocheons
July the 16th 1705 at St Bridgets Church Dublin, She was
wife to Sr Frances Blundell Bart And Daughter to Sr Henry
Ingolsby Bart.

**Dame FitsGerald** wife to Donolan was Intered January the 12<sup>th</sup> 1705 with Scocheons.

(703)
(Arms.)
Donolan
Fitz-
Gerrald.

**Captain Henry Dodwell** Esq<sup>r</sup> was Interred at Athlone Aprill y<sup>e</sup> 24<sup>th</sup> 1707 with Scocheons   He married M<sup>rs</sup> Daughter of Ormsby and had by her 3 Daughters.

Page 349.
(704)
(Arms.)
Dodwell :
Ormsby.

The armes of Henry Dodwell Esq<sup>r</sup>

(Arms.)
Dodwell.
(705)

**Coll-Jeffers** of Castle Jordan Com- of                          was Interred June the 12<sup>th</sup> 1707 with Scocheons.

(706)
(Arms.)
Jeffers.

**Coll-Warneford** was Interred at Mount Mellick August the 8<sup>th</sup> 1707 with Scocheons.

(707)
(Arms.)
Warneford

**Nathaniell Foy Alias De Foix** by Divine Providence Late Lord Bishop of Waterford he Departed this Life In Dublin January the 1<sup>st</sup> 1707 and was Interred In Waterford with Scocheons.

(708)
(Arms.)
Foye als
De foix.

The above armes of Foy late Lord bishop of Waterford and Lismore are here Impaled with the ancient See of Waterford.

(709)
(Arms.)
See of
Waterfd
Foye.

**Captain Archer** Com̃. Wicklow was Interred March y<sup>e</sup> 14<sup>th</sup> 1707<sup>8</sup> with Scocheons.

age 350.
P (710)
(Arms.)
Archer.

**William Naper** Esq<sup>r</sup> Departed This Life In Dublin May y<sup>e</sup> 20<sup>th</sup> 1708 and was Interred at Loghcreew with Escocheons and 2 Hathments one for y<sup>e</sup> church other y<sup>e</sup> outside of y<sup>e</sup> House and 2 pennos In y<sup>e</sup> church.   Crest an Armd arm Couped at y<sup>e</sup> Shoulders Grasping a Cressant G.

(711)
(Arms.)
Napper.

**Edward Brabazon Earle of meath** whose first wife was M<sup>rs</sup> Cecilia Daughter of Sir William Brereton of Cheshire second Wife by y<sup>e</sup> Name of Stopford.

(712)
(Arms.)
Brabazon.

**The Hon<sup>ble</sup> Edward Brabazon** Earle of meath was Interred at S<sup>t</sup> Katherines Church Dublin, whose second Wife was M<sup>rs</sup> Dorothy Daughter of Coll. James Stopford.   He was Buried February the 26<sup>th</sup> 1708 with Scocheons.

(713)
(Arms.)
Brabazon
Stopford.

(714)       **The Hon<sup>ble</sup> Lady Elizabeth Boyle** Daughter of Roger
(Arms.)  Earle of Orrory  She was married to the Hon<sup>ble</sup> Folliot
**Wingfield**  Wingfield Ld. Visc<sup>t</sup> Powerscourt and was Intered under the
**Boyle.**  Communion Table att S<sup>t</sup> Patricks Church Dublin on y<sup>e</sup> 23<sup>d</sup> of
October 1709 with Scocheons.

(715)      **The Hon Elizabeth Lady Powerscourt** Daughter to
(Arms.)  the Hon<sup>ble</sup> Roger Boyle Earle of Orrory.
**Boyle.**

**Page 351.**
(716)      These are the arms of Captain Henry Monk of S<sup>t</sup> Stephens
(Arms.)  Green.
**Monke.**

(717)      **Captain Henry Monk** of S<sup>t</sup> Stephens Green he married
(Arms.)  M<sup>rs</sup> Sarah Daughter of S<sup>r</sup> Thomas Stanley  He was Interred
**Monk :**  In S<sup>t</sup> Michans Vaults on Aprill the 8<sup>th</sup> 1710
**Stanley.**  with Scocheons.

(718)      **Captain May** was Interred att           Church
(Arms.)  Aprill The 11<sup>th</sup> 1710 with Scocheons  [Crest a talbots
**May.**  erasd A] *
*In pencil.

(719)      **Cornall Donolan** was Interred Jully The 10<sup>th</sup> 1710 with
(Arms.)  Scocheons.
**Donolan.**

(720)      **Mr Maugan** Com̃. West Meath was Interred at
(Arms.)            Church september the 8<sup>th</sup> 1710
**Mangan.**  with Scocheons.

(721)      **Mrs Bingham** ma<sup>d</sup> to M<sup>r</sup> Robert Bell  She was Interred
(Arms)  at            Church october y<sup>e</sup> 8<sup>th</sup> 1710 with
**Bell :**
**Bingham.**  Scocheons.

(722)      **The Hon<sup>ble</sup> Peirce Lord Visc<sup>t</sup> Ikerine** whose
(Arms.)  first wife was Madam Alicia Boyle Daughter to y<sup>e</sup>
**Butle<sup>r</sup> Boyle of**  Hon<sup>ble</sup> Morogh Boyle L<sup>d</sup> Visc<sup>t</sup> Blessinton.
**Blessington 1<sup>st</sup> wife.**

The following is on a page inserted between ff. 351 and
352 (*see Certificate No.* 724).

Funerall of y<sup>e</sup> Rig<sup>t</sup> Hon<sup>ble</sup> Peirce Lord Vis<sup>ct</sup> Ikerine from
Bally Lynch to Thomas towne January y<sup>e</sup> 4<sup>th</sup> 17$\frac{10}{11}$

    1<sup>st</sup> Troope of Horss
    2<sup>dly</sup> 2 Conductors On foote
    3<sup>d</sup> Esq<sup>r</sup> Freaks Serv<sup>ts</sup> 2 : & 2

4<sup>th</sup> Esq<sup>r</sup> Freaks Led Horss
5<sup>th</sup> 2 Conductors, on foote
6<sup>th</sup> Lords, Serv<sup>ts</sup> 2 : 2
7<sup>th</sup> Lords Led Horss all in black with Scocheons
8<sup>th</sup> 2 Conductors, on foote
9<sup>th</sup> More Serv<sup>ts</sup> 2 & 2
10<sup>th</sup> Cooke & Buttler
11<sup>th</sup> State Horss all in black with Shaffroons, Feathers, Scocheons, &c.
12<sup>th</sup> Steward, & Comptroler with white Rodds
13<sup>th</sup> Gentleman with Sword [Cornet George Butler] *
14<sup>th</sup> Chaplins – 6 or 8
15<sup>th</sup> Crowne Carried on a Cushion
16<sup>th</sup> Herss with 6 Horses
17<sup>th</sup> Cheif Mourners In black Coaches
18<sup>th</sup> Other Relations 2 & 2 all on Horssback
19<sup>th</sup> Coaches &c.

These are the armes of the Hon<sup>ble</sup> L<sup>d</sup> Visc<sup>t</sup> Ikerine.

Page 352.
(723)
(Arms.)
Buttler.

The Hon<sup>ble</sup> Peirce L<sup>d</sup> Visc<sup>t</sup> Ikerine was Interred from his House att Bally Lynch Com Killkenny His Second wife was Mad<sup>m</sup> Olivia S<sup>t</sup> Gorge Daugt<sup>r</sup> to The Hon<sup>ble</sup> S<sup>r</sup> Oliver S<sup>t</sup> Gorge He was Buried att Thomas Towne with Scocheons January y<sup>e</sup> 4<sup>th</sup> 1710 He Died at Castle Freake Com. Cork.

(724)
(Arms.)
Butler 2d
wife St.
George.

The Hon<sup>ble</sup> S<sup>r</sup> Peirce Meade Bart. was Interred In Christe Church — Dublinn Jully the 18<sup>th</sup> 1711 with Scocheons

(725)
(Arms.)
Meade.

The Hon<sup>ble</sup> Rich<sup>d</sup> Boyle * Esq<sup>r</sup> whose first wife was M<sup>rs</sup> Savage daughter to Sauage.

(726)
(Arms.)
Boyle:
Savage
1st wife.

The Armes of Rich<sup>d</sup> Boyle Esq<sup>r</sup>

(727)
(Arms.)
Boyle.

The Hon<sup>ble</sup> Rich<sup>d</sup> Boyle * Esq<sup>r</sup> was Interred in S<sup>t</sup> Warboroughs Church vaults November 24<sup>th</sup> 1711 with Scocheons ; his Second wife was Mad<sup>:m</sup> Rebecca Bellingham Daughter of S<sup>r</sup> Daniell Bellingham K<sup>t</sup> Bart. 1<sup>st</sup> Lord mayor of Dublin.

(728)
(Arms.)
Boyle :
Daugtr of
Sr. Daniell
Bellinghm
2d wife.

These are the armes of S<sup>t</sup> Gorge S<sup>t</sup> Gorge of Smith feild

Page 353.
(729)
(Arms.)
St. George

---

* Son of Dr. Richard Boyle, Bishop of Ferns and Leighlin, who died in 1682.

16

(730)     The Hon<sup>ble</sup> S<sup>r</sup> George S<sup>t</sup> George from Smith feild
(Arms.)   was Interred in Christs Church December The 3<sup>d</sup> 1711 with
St George: Scocheons. his Second wife was Elizabeth Daugh<sup>r</sup> to S<sup>r</sup>
Hannah.   Robert Hannah of Scotland.
*In pencil.

(731)     M<sup>r</sup> Wilcocks [formerly a Quaker] * Com̃ of  —  was
(Arms.)   Interred att mount melick with Scocheons January the
Willcocks. 12<sup>th</sup> 1711.

(732)     The Hon<sup>ble</sup> Livetennant Generrall Langston's
(Arms.)   Daughter was Interred (afrom S<sup>t</sup> Stephen green) In S<sup>t</sup>
Langstone  Peeters Church Aprill y<sup>e</sup> 24<sup>th</sup> 1712 with Escocheons.

(733)     M<sup>rs</sup> Brilliana Rawden had Scocheons Painted october
(Arms.)   y<sup>e</sup> 11. 1712 but by W<sup>m</sup> Hawkins treachery they were not mad
Rawden.   use of.

(734)     The Rev<sup>erd</sup> father In god John Pooley L<sup>d</sup> Bishopp
(Arms.)   of Raphoe was Interred at S<sup>t</sup> Michans Church october y<sup>e</sup> 19<sup>th</sup>
See of    1712 w<sup>th</sup> Scocheons whose arms are here Impaled with the
Raphoe    Saee of Raphoe.
Pooley.

Page 354.
(735)     O'Toole als Tooley Or Touhill was Interd In the
(Arms.)   County of Wicklow with Scocheons.
Toole.

(736)     Batty was Interrd with Scocheons January The Twenty
(Arms.)   Eighth . . . 1711          . . .
Batty.

(737)     Captain Smith of Drum Cree was Interred October the
(Arms.)   30<sup>th</sup> 1712 with Scocheons.
Smith.

(738)     Capt<sup>n</sup>     Smith was married to
(Arms.)   Mrs     Hatfield  he was buried at Drumcree In The Com̃
Smith :   Westmeath.
Hatfeild.

(739)     M<sup>r</sup> Desper May the 8<sup>th</sup> 1713 was Interred near Mount-
(Arms.)   rath with Scocheons              november y<sup>e</sup> 20<sup>th</sup> 1716
Desper.   painted 8 silk Escocheons and 42 paper ditto for y<sup>e</sup> s<sup>d</sup> Despers
          Family.

---

* [Of Carlow]

M<sup>rs</sup> **Hinton** married to         Bunbury Esq<sup>r</sup> * was    (740)
Interred with Scocheons Jully y<sup>e</sup> 1<sup>st</sup> 1713        (Arms.)
Beyond Carlow —   —   —   —        Bunbury :
       Hinton.

     **Dame Ann Eustace** married to Benjamen Chetwood Page 355.
Esq<sup>r</sup> She was Daught<sup>r</sup> and heir of S<sup>r</sup> Morris Eustace and    (741)
was Interred att S<sup>t</sup> Bridgetts Church August y<sup>e</sup> 17<sup>th</sup> 1713   (Arms.)
with Scocheons        Chettwood:
       Eustace.

     M<sup>rs</sup> **Vigours** Daught<sup>r</sup> to Bartholomew Vigours L<sup>d</sup> Bishopp   (742)
of ferns and Laughlin   She was married to S<sup>t</sup> Leger Gilbert   (Arms.)
and was Interred in S<sup>t</sup> Patricks Church Dublin September y<sup>e</sup>   Gillbert :
20<sup>th</sup> 1713 with Schocheons.        Vigours.

     The Hon<sup>ble.</sup> S<sup>r</sup> **Francis Hamilton Barronett** was    (743)
Interred att Killishandra In the County of Cavan February   (Arms.)
the 9<sup>th</sup> 1713 with Scocheons        Hamilton.

     This Arms is thus Blazond.   G 3  ⊕ ⋏ ¼ tred with Ld
Semple of Scotland (viz<sup>t</sup>)   A a ∧ checky G & of y<sup>e</sup> 1st·
entr 3 bugle Horns S. Garnished of y<sup>e</sup> 2<sup>d</sup> Impaled with G 3.5
foils ⋏ & bart. Hand, Crest a tree pr on a Wreath thrust
thro with a Sword wavy pr. over it on an Escroll.   Solo in
Cœlum.

     **Dame Dorothy Hall** was married to M<sup>r</sup>    Bayly of      (744)
and was Interred In S<sup>t</sup> Michaels Church Dublin march the   (Arms.)
5<sup>th</sup> 17$\frac{14}{13}$ w<sup>th</sup> Scocheons        Bayly
       Hall.

     ·**Docter Mathew French** a Seiniour fellow of Trinity   (745)
Colledge Dublin was Interred In the Chappell of the S<sup>d</sup>   (Arms.)
Colledge march The 13<sup>th</sup> 17$\frac{14}{13}$ with Scocheons        French.

     M<sup>rs</sup> **Euphalia Mervin** Daughter to Audley Mervin of   (746)
the Naall Esq<sup>r</sup> She was Interrd within 2 mile of y<sup>e</sup> s<sup>d</sup>   (Arms.)
Naall y<sup>e</sup> 15<sup>th</sup> of January 1714 with Escocheons — —     Mervin.

     The R<sup>t</sup> Hon<sup>ble</sup> **Catherine Countess of Granard** Page 356.
was first married to Sir Alexander Stewart, Secondly She   (747)
was married to arthur Forbes Earle of Granard ; She was the   (Arms.)
Daughter of Sir Robert Newcomen and was Interd at     Forbes
with Scocheons y<sup>e</sup> 13<sup>th</sup> of December 1714 and Lay In State   Newcomen
In Dublin before She was Carried to y<sup>e</sup> Country   At which
time by Sad Accident the Lady Sands was burnt to Death In
her own chamber.

---

* Of Killerrig, Co. Carlow.

(748)
(Arms.)
Capt.
Thomas
Hickman.

**Cap<sup>tn</sup> Thomas Hickman** Son of         Hickman
from his Lodgings In Dames Street to S<sup>t</sup> Warboroughs
Church the 9<sup>th</sup> of February 1714 with Scocheons — — — —

(749)
(Arms.)

O'Reily | Butler
ought to | on this
be on this | side.
side. |

**Mrs Emelia, Daughter to Edmund Buttler**
L<sup>d</sup> **Mountgarrett** She was married to Hugh
O'Reiley Esq<sup>r</sup> & Interd at Ballynlough Com west
meath, with Scocheons—May the 6<sup>th</sup> 1715.

(750)
(Arms.)
Jones:
Meade.

**Thomas Jones** Esq<sup>r</sup> married m<sup>rs</sup> meade Daughter To S<sup>r</sup>
John meade Bar<sup>t</sup> Interd at y<sup>e</sup> Church In y<sup>e</sup> Naas with
Scocheons July the 11<sup>th</sup> 1715.

(751)
(Arms.)
Hackett.

**Mrs Hackett** Interrd at wicklow with Scocheons —
July 15<sup>th</sup> 1715.

(752)
(Arms.)
Monk
Stanley.

**Mrs Sarah Daughter of S<sup>r</sup> Tho: Stanley K<sup>nt</sup>** Some-
time of Grange Gorman Near Dublin ; She was married To
Cap<sup>tn</sup> Henry Monk and was Interd In the vaults of new
S<sup>t</sup> michans Church Oxmontown y<sup>e</sup> 23<sup>d</sup> of August 1715 with
Scocheons —      —      —      —

Page 357.
(753)
See of
Meat<sup>h</sup>
Moreton.
(Arms.)

**The Reverend Father In God Will<sup>m</sup> Moreton** of an
antient family In Cheshire by Devine Providence Lord
Bishopp of Meath He Marrried the Relict of Arthur Jones
K<sup>t</sup> he was Interrd In Christs Church Vaults November y<sup>e</sup> 24.
1715.

(754)
(Arms.)
Willson:
Waters.

**Ralph Willson** Esq<sup>r</sup> he married m<sup>rs</sup> Waters and was
Interrd at S<sup>t</sup> Marys Church with Scocheons   —   December
y<sup>e</sup> 19<sup>th</sup> 1715   —   —   —

(755)
(Arms.)
Bunbary :
Huband.

**Benjamen Bunbury**\* Esq<sup>r</sup> Interd In the County of
Carlow with Scocheons y<sup>e</sup> 6<sup>th</sup> of January 1715 he married
m<sup>rs</sup>      Daughter of Huband —   —

(756)
(Arms.)
Ashe:
St. George.

**The Reverend Doct<sup>r</sup> Dillon Ashe** he was Interd at
finglas near Dublin he married Eliz: Daughter of S<sup>r</sup> George
S<sup>t</sup> George he was Interd with Scocheons May y<sup>e</sup> 18<sup>th</sup> 1716.
This Dillon Ashe was brother to the Reverend S<sup>t</sup> George
Ashe Lord Bishopp of Derry who was Interd at Christs
Church.

---

\* Of Killerrig, Co. Carlow.

M<sup>rs</sup> **Daughter to Tannat** of Chester  She was (757)
Married to  M<sup>r</sup>  Hackett of Wicklow  She was Interd (Arms.)
with Escocheons December y<sup>e</sup> 28<sup>th</sup> 1716 —  —  — Hackett :
Tannat.

**The Hon<sup>ble</sup> Thomas Moore** Son & heir to the R<sup>t</sup> ' (758)
Hon<sup>ble</sup> John Moore L<sup>d</sup> Barron of Tullamore In the Kings | (Arms.)
County.  he was Interd at Croughan with Scocheons Pencills Moor'.
body In Railes and Canopy, with Majesty Scocheons, &c.
May y<sup>e</sup> 10<sup>th</sup> 1717.

**Audley Mervin Esq<sup>r</sup>** of The Naall  he married Page 358.
M<sup>rs</sup>  Coote Daughter of  Coote and (759)
was Interd In Christ Church Vaults with Scocheons (Arms )
June y<sup>e</sup> 18<sup>th</sup> 1717 — — — Mervin  Impaled
with Coote : Viz<sup>t</sup> A
a ∧ Inter 3 Cootes S.

**Barry** of  he was Interrd at  In the County (760)
of West meath with Scocheons January the 30<sup>th</sup> 1717 — — (Arms.)
Barry.

**Francis Power** Esq<sup>r</sup> married m<sup>rs</sup> Elizabeth Quartermain (761)
He was Killed by  Dayly and Interrd at Loughrea with (Arms.)
Escocheons February the 21<sup>st</sup> 1717 — — — — y<sup>e</sup> Power
crest of s<sup>d</sup> ffrancis a Staggs head sable Couped colired or. Quarter-
maine.

. **M<sup>rs</sup> Blithe** Married to Thomas Ash Esq<sup>r</sup>  She was (762)
Interd at the Church of Trim with Scocheons February The (Arms.)
24<sup>th</sup> 1717 — — — Ash<sup>e</sup> :
Blythe.

**M<sup>rs</sup> Faye** Daughter of  She Married Colt Hamilton (763)
and was Interrd at Dunboyne Church with Scocheons Aprill (Arms.)
y<sup>e</sup> 1<sup>st</sup> 1718 — — Hamilton :
Faye.

**M<sup>rs</sup> Ann Daughter of  Kent** She married Docter (764)
Daniell Gates  She was Carried from her Lodgings In (Arms.)
Thomas Street at Mc Clintons to y<sup>e</sup> Parish Church of Yates or
S<sup>t</sup> Paules and was there Interrd with Scocheons the 20<sup>th</sup> of Gates :
May the Said Daniell Gates was Docter of Phisick  1718 Kent.

**John Pearcivall** Esq<sup>r</sup> of Knights Brook Page 359.
in the County of Meath  he Married an heires (765)
he was Intered at the Parish Church of Percivall married to an
Larahour near Trim with Scocheons October heires y<sup>e</sup> Hors charged with
the 24<sup>th</sup> 1718.  the Crest of this Coat is the a scocheon of Pretence per
same as y<sup>e</sup> Arms. fess or & sable 3 Griffins
Sergret or

**M<sup>rs</sup> Twigg** wife of Counceller Twigg & Daugter to (766)
Purefoy  She was Interrd at S<sup>t</sup> Kavans Church with (Arms.)
Scocheons  November y<sup>e</sup> 18<sup>th</sup> 1718 — — — Twigg :
Purefoy.

(767)
(Arms.)
Coote:
King.

**Coll: Coote** of Cootehill was Interr'd with Scocheons In the Said Church Aprill the 25<sup>th</sup> 1719   he Married M<sup>rs</sup> King Daughter of              &c.

(768)
(Arms.)
Irwin.

The Proceeding of the Funerall of M<sup>rs</sup> Alice Irwin to S<sup>t</sup> Bridgetts Church 25<sup>th</sup> of May 1719.   From william Street her lodgings.

1<sup>st</sup> y<sup>e</sup> Beadle of the Parish
  2 Conductors
2<sup>dly</sup> y<sup>e</sup> Parish Boys 2 & 2
3<sup>dly</sup> two Conductors
4<sup>thly</sup> y<sup>e</sup> Porter of y<sup>e</sup> blew boys
5<sup>thly</sup> y<sup>e</sup> Blew boys 2 & 2
6<sup>thly</sup> y<sup>e</sup> Master of the blew boys
7<sup>th</sup> two Conductors
8<sup>th</sup> men Serv<sup>ts</sup> 2 & 2
9<sup>th</sup> Women Serv<sup>ts</sup> 2 & 2
10<sup>th</sup> two Conductors
  Docter and Apothecary
11<sup>th</sup> the clergy next the
  Body two & two

12<sup>th</sup> Herse Drawne by 6 Horsses all Cover'd with black, & white feathers On their heads and Lead by 6 Men In black, the Herss adorn'd with white feathers, Vellvett Valloons, fur belong d with white Sarcenett, y<sup>e</sup> Body Cover'd with Vellvett Pall, fur belong'd with white Sarcenett, & 4 Plumes of white feathers in y<sup>e</sup> Herss about the body, The Pall bore up by Six Young Ladies, with white hoods Scarves and Gloves &c.
13<sup>th</sup> Relations In Mourning 2 & 2
14<sup>th</sup> Gentlemen with Scarves 2 & 2
15<sup>th</sup> Gentlemens Coaches

Page 360.
(769)
(Arms.)
: Cooley.

**Henry Cooley** Esq<sup>r</sup> was Interrd at Castle Carbury In the County of Kildare, July the 4<sup>th</sup> 1719, with Scocheons

Crest a
Stags Head
Caboshd G.
(770)
(Arms.)
Wakely.

M<sup>r</sup> **William Weakly** was Interd In the Church of Bally-burly In the Kings County, September the 17<sup>th</sup> 1719 with Scocheons.

(771)
(Arms.)
St.George:
Eyres.

M<sup>rs</sup> **Eyres** was Interd In the Cathedrall of Christ Church Novemb<sup>r</sup> y<sup>e</sup> 27<sup>th</sup> 1719 with Scocheons   She was mary<sup>d</sup> to Coll. S<sup>t</sup> George &c.  —  ·—  —  —

(772) (1)
(Arms.)
See of
Elphin.
Digby.

**Essex Digby L<sup>d</sup> Bishop of Dromore,** married m<sup>rs.</sup> Gilbert, by her had 3 Sons, will<sup>m</sup> Robert & Simon.
This Simon was Consecrated L<sup>d</sup> Bishop of Limerick, Ardfert, & Aghadoe, 19 march, 1678 : 30 Charles 2<sup>d</sup> Trans-lated to Elphin the 12<sup>th</sup> of January 1691 : 3<sup>d</sup> of Will : & Mary ; he married m<sup>rs</sup> Elizabeth Westenra Daug̃. of Warner Westenra

& by her had Issue Tomasin; Robert; Elizabeth, she mar^d
to y^e Rev^rd Jeremy marsh Deane of Killmore and by her had
one Son Jeremy and One Daugh^r; Frances; Simon; Lettice;
margreat; Henry; Abigall; all Sans Issue.

4^th John he mar̃: m^rs mary marsh, Daugh: to y^e Rev^rd
Jeremy marsh, by a Daugh: of Henry Dodwell Esq^r
Mary Westenray 2^d Son Jane mar̃: to Patrick French Coucill-
at-Law Com̃: Gallway, Will^m, Essex Gilbert, Benjamin, &
Rebeckagh, all Unmari^d  The above Simon, Lord Bishop of
Elphin Departed this Life at his House Call'd Lackan, in the
County of Roscomon in y^e Province of Connaght on Thursday
the 7^th of Aprill 1720, and on Friday the 15^th following being
Good friday, his Lady Elizabeth Westenray Departed, and
were both Interrd, at one time, in one Herss, one Vault, and
one Funerall Sermon on Wednesday the 20^th of y^e same month,
in y^e Church of Tosrara in the S^d County with Funerall
Solemnities.

(772) (2)
(Arms.)
Digby
Westen-
ray.

| | |
|---|---|
| 1 Robert | 1 Tomasin |
| 2 Simon | 2 Elizabeth |
| 3 Henry | 3 Lettice |
| 4 John | 4 margreat |
| 5 Westenray | 5 Abigall |
| 6 Will^m | 6 mary |
| 7 Essex | 7 Jane |
| 8 Gilbert | 8 Rebeckah |
| 9 Benjamin | |

M^r             Nevill Thursday Jully y^e 28. 1720. Page 361.
Interd at ForeNaass * w^th 8 Silk Scocheons for y^e body, 26
mettall for Herse and Horses, & 6 shaffrions for y^e Horses
Heads by Henry Hodgshkinson

(773)
(Arms.)
Nevill
Barry.

Blew a Lyon Rampant or by the name of King;
Ermine a Cheveron Gules by y^e name of French, County of
Roscommon; Scocheons Painted y^e 26^th & Inter'd y^e 29^th of
December 1720 in Connaught.

(774)
(Arms.)
King:
French.

Thomas Bernard Deceas'd. may the 2^d in the County
of Carlow Gent. and was Interd there the 5^th Day 1721. with
Scocheons.

(775)
(Arms.)
Bernard.

Scocheons Painted for M^r     .     .     .     the 29^th Day
of December 1721.

(776)
(Arms.)
Gayner
Every.

* Furness, Co. Kildare.

**Page 362.**
(777)
(Arms.)
Mervin.

**James Mervin** 3<sup>d</sup> Son of Audley Mervin of the Naall Esq<sup>r</sup> was Inter'd in y<sup>e</sup> Church of Clonmaiden February the 11<sup>th</sup> 1721 with Scocheons

(778)
(Arms.)
Butler.

**Jordan Butler** Son of S<sup>r</sup> Toby Butler Councill at Law, he was Inter'd at S<sup>t</sup> James's Church Dublin March y<sup>e</sup> 2<sup>d</sup> 1721-22 ; with Scocheons for Herse Horses & Body

(779)
(Arms.)
Tisdall
Boyle.

**M<sup>rs</sup> Mary Tisdall** Daughter to Richard Boyle Esq<sup>r</sup> by M<sup>rs</sup> Savage Daughter to Valentine Savage of y<sup>e</sup> Citty of Dublin Gent ; She was Inter'd in y<sup>e</sup> Parish Church of Finglass neere Dublin with Funerall Solemnities &c. She was marry'd to Richard Tisdall Esq<sup>r</sup> Sometime Clark of y<sup>e</sup> Crown Dublin Aprill y<sup>e</sup> 29<sup>th</sup> 1722

(780)
(Arms.)
Fielding.

**The Hon<sup>ble</sup> S<sup>r</sup> Charles Fielding** Aged 79 years, 4<sup>th</sup> Son of the Hon<sup>ble</sup> Earl of Desmond and Denbigh, he was Knighted about the year 1673, he being one of y<sup>e</sup> Rangers of his Majesties Park neere Dublin and governor of y<sup>e</sup> Royall Hospitall neere Kilmainham, & Liev<sup>t</sup> Colonell to y<sup>e</sup> Royall Regiment of foot in King Charles y<sup>e</sup> 2<sup>ds</sup> Days, and one of the Honble Privy Councill of y<sup>e</sup> s<sup>d</sup> Kingdome of Ireland, he Deceased in Aprill —— 1722 & was Inter'd y<sup>e</sup> 27<sup>th</sup> in S<sup>t</sup> Michaells Church Dublin, w<sup>th</sup> funerall Solemnities, (viz<sup>t</sup>) Escocheons for y<sup>e</sup> body Herse & Horses, and was attended by y<sup>e</sup> Children of 3 Charity Schools & the Blew Hospitall boy's thus, Impr, 3 beadles 2 Conductors master and boys of S<sup>t</sup> marys Parish, 2<sup>d</sup>, 2 Conductors master & boys of S<sup>t</sup> Michans, 3<sup>d</sup> 2 Conductors master & Parish boys of S<sup>t</sup> Michealls, 4<sup>th</sup> 2 Conductors, master, Porter, & blew boys of y<sup>e</sup> Hospitall, 6 Carriers in Gown's before 10 Servants in Cloaks & y<sup>e</sup> Horse, &c.

(781)
(Arms.)
Stewart.

**The Arms of** Cap<sup>t</sup> Rob<sup>t</sup> Stewart as they are erected in y<sup>e</sup> Parish Church of Castle Ruddrey in y<sup>e</sup> County of Wicklow who was inter'd in y<sup>e</sup> S<sup>d</sup> Church & built by him, Originally of y<sup>e</sup> family of L<sup>d</sup> O Chiltree.

**Page 363.**
(782)
(Arms.)
Stewart.

**Cap<sup>t</sup> Robert Stewart** was Interd at the Parish Church of Castle Ruddrey y<sup>e</sup>  Day of  1722 with Escocheons &c.

(783)
(Arms.)
Wakely.

**M<sup>rs</sup> Arebella Wakely** 6<sup>th</sup> Daughter of Esq<sup>r</sup> John Wakely of Bally Burly was Interd at y<sup>e</sup> S<sup>d</sup> Church y<sup>e</sup> 18<sup>th</sup> Day of November 1722 with Escocheons &c.

**John Drury** Esq<sup>r</sup>. was Interd from Meath Street to St Michans Church Dublin y<sup>e</sup> 11 Day of December 1722 with Escocheons &c.

(784)
(Arms.)
Drury.

**Mrs Catherine Cox** Daughter of S<sup>r</sup> Richard Cox Bar<sup>t</sup> & wife of Counc<sup>ll</sup> Moore Esq<sup>r</sup> Son of Coĺĺ Roger Moore  She was Intered at y<sup>e</sup> Church of Finglass y<sup>e</sup> 15<sup>th</sup> Day of Aprill 1723 with Escocheons &c.

(785)
(Arms.)
Moore Cox.

**Cap<sup>t</sup> Arthur Stewart** 4<sup>h</sup> Brõ to y<sup>e</sup> Lord Visc<sup>t</sup> Mountjoy he was Interd from his Lodgings in Smith field to Church y<sup>e</sup>      Day of          1723 with Escocheons &c.

(786)
(Arms.)
Stewart.

(Certificate in pencil—now illegible.)

(787)
(Arms.)

**Mrs Catherine Wakely** wife of Lewis Meare's Esq<sup>r</sup>. was Inter'd at Meares-Court the 6<sup>th</sup> Day of          1723 with Escocheons &c.

Page 364.
(788)
(Arms.)
Meares
Wakely.

**Mrs . . . Young** wife of Major Pieter Verdoen She was Inter'd at S<sup>t</sup> Mary's Church Dublin y<sup>e</sup>      Day of 1723 with Escocheons &c.

(789)
(Arms.)
Verdoen
Young.

**Coll Andrew Armstrong*** was Interd from Morristown, County Kildare to y<sup>e</sup> Church of Old Connell, y<sup>e</sup> Day of          1723 in the County of Killdare with Escocheons &c.

(790)
(Arms.)
Armstrong

These are the Arms of Cap<sup>t</sup> Townley.

(791)
(Arms.)
Townley.

**Cap<sup>t</sup> — Townley** mar<sup>d</sup> M<sup>rs</sup>      Moyne, he was Inter'd at the Church of Navan — Dec. 25<sup>th</sup> 1724 with Escocheons &c.

(792)
(Arms.)
Townley
Moyne.

**Counc<sup>ll</sup> Blennar Hasset** Died at his Lodgings in fishamble Street Dublin, & was Interd at S<sup>t</sup> John's Church June 9<sup>th</sup> 1724.

(793)
(Arms.)
Blenr-
hasset.

3 Roses Arg<sup>t</sup> seeded or.

Page 365.
A on ∧ S.

---

* Third son of Edmund, ancestor of Sir Andrew H. Armstrong, Bart., of Gallen Priory, King's County (see Burke).

(794)
(Arms.)
Gilbert.
Ye Roses
are to be
on ye
cheveron.

Mrs Gertrude Gilbert Dau. of Co<sup>ll</sup> Gilbert Died at her Lodgings in Peter Street & was Interd at y<sup>e</sup> Cathedral Church of S<sup>t</sup> Patrick Dublin, thirsday July 2<sup>d</sup> 1724 with Escocheons &c.

(795)
(Arms.)
Lee.

Robert Lee Esq<sup>r</sup> of Rathbride was Interd In y<sup>e</sup> County Carlowe Wednesday October 2<sup>d</sup> 1724.

(796)
(Arms.)
Ponsoby.

The R<sup>t</sup> Hon<sup>ble</sup> L<sup>d</sup> Visc<sup>t</sup> Besborough Died at his house            & was Interd at Novemb<sup>r</sup> 20<sup>th</sup> 1724 with Escocheons.

(797)
(Arms not
tricked.)
Shean.

The Hon<sup>ble</sup> S<sup>r</sup> Arthur Shean who mar. M<sup>rs</sup> Magan was Interd at            June y<sup>e</sup> 28<sup>th</sup> 1725 w<sup>th</sup> funerall Solemnities.

(798)
(Arms not
tricked.)
Clayton.

The Rev<sup>d</sup> Dean Clayton Died at his house in Church Street & was Interd in S<sup>t</sup> Michans Church Dublin Sep<sup>t</sup> 26<sup>th</sup> 1725 w<sup>th</sup> funerall Solemnities—where M<sup>r</sup> Crossly by falling into a Celler gott his Death—died 8<sup>ber</sup> 1<sup>st</sup> 1725.

Page 366.
(799)
(Arms.)
Berry
Smith.

Eschocheons Painted for Cor<sup>ll</sup> Berry 8<sup>ber</sup> y<sup>e</sup> 9<sup>th</sup> 1725 Impailed w<sup>th</sup> Smith.

(800)
(Arms.)
Dixon.

Co<sup>ll</sup> Rob<sup>t</sup> Dixon of Calverstowne County Kildare was Interd at y<sup>e</sup> Church of Kilcullin from his Lodgings at y<sup>e</sup> upper End of Jervis Street on Wednesday March 9<sup>th</sup> 172⅚ w<sup>th</sup> Scocheons &c.

(801)
(Arms not
tricked.)
Savage.

Wednesday March 30<sup>th</sup> Painted Escocheons for Esq<sub>r</sub> Savage who was brought from London & Inter'd at Portaferry Saturday Aprill 2<sup>d</sup> 1726 w<sup>th</sup> funerall Solemnities.

(802)
(Arms.)
Warren.

Wednesday June 1<sup>t</sup> M<sup>r</sup> Mau. Warren of Grangebegg County Kildare died at his Lodgings on Ormond Key & was Intered at            w<sup>th</sup> Escocheons &c June 2<sup>d</sup> 1726.

(803)
(Arms.)
Monk
Ponsonby.

Geo: Monks of S<sup>t</sup> Stephans Green Esq<sup>r</sup> who Mar: Ponsoby was Interred at S<sup>t</sup> Michans Church on thirsday 28<sup>th</sup> July 1726 w<sup>th</sup> funerall Solemnities &c.

(804)
(Arms not
tricked.)
Donolan
Wentworth

Donolan Esq<sup>r</sup> who Mar<sup>d</sup>            Wentworth Died at his Lodgins in Liffey Street & was Interred at Cavan Church 3<sup>d</sup> of August 1726 w<sup>th</sup> funerall Solemnities &c.

**Donolan Esq^r** who Mar^d Dillon Died at his Lodgins in fleet Street & was Interred at Cavan 29^th of Nov^r 1726 w^th Escocheons &c.

Page 367.
(805)
(Arms not tricked.)
Donolan
Dillon.

**In° Townley** Esq^r aged 12 years, Son of Cap^t Townley of Navan Died at his Lodgings in Castle Street & was Interr'd at Navan on Saturday 17^th Jan^ry 172$\frac{6}{7}$ with Escocheons &c.

(806)
(Arms.)
Townley.

**M^rs Jane Lee** Wife of Christ^r Johnson Esq^r Died at his house at Killternon and was Inter'd at S^t Kevans Church on Sunday 23^d of Aprill 1727 with Funerall Solemnities.

(807)
(Arms not tricked.)
Van
Janson or
Johnson
Lee.

**Maurice Keating** of Narramore Esq^r who mar: M^rs . . . Margretson. Died at his house afores^d on thirsday 4^th May 1727, and was Inter'd there Monday following w^th funeral Solemnities.

(808)
(Arms.)
Keating
Margret-
son.

**Miss Eliz: Dau^r of Coll Dawson** Died at her Lodgins in York Street & was Inter'd at S^t Paul's Church Dub. 7^th feb. 172$\frac{8}{9}$ w^th fun^ll Solemnities & some small time after was taken up & Carried to her fa^rs Mansion Seat near Limerick.

(809)
(Arms.)
Dawson.

**M^r Anthony Cliff** Died at his Lodgins in Bride Street & was Interd at Clongulf* in y^e County Wexford 3^d Dec. 1729. With funerall Solemnities.

(810)
(Arms.)
Cliff.

**John Ivers** Esq^r Died at his house at S^t Stephans Green and was Inter'd at S^t Peters Church Dublin the 4^th December 1729 w^th Funerall Solemnities.

Page 368.
(811)
(Arms.)
Ivers.

**Abigail Daur. of Cap^t Thos. Smith** of Drumcree and Wife of Thomas Judge of Grange begg County West meath Esq^r She died at Grange begg aforesaid march y^e 2^nd 1726 and was Inter'd the Sunday following at Drumcree w^th fun^ll Solemnities, This ought to be Enter'd after Coll. Rob^t Dixon.

(812)
(Arms not tricked.)
Judge
Smith.

See No. (800). (From here to page 525 is blank.)

**Elizabeth daughter of S^r James weyms Knt & of** Judith daughter of S^r William Usher Knt. departed this mortall life unmaried at Dublin the 19 day of Jully 1688 being the 21 year of her age. She was interred the 21 of the same month in the Tomb or buriall place belonging to Xpher

Page 526.
(813)

---

* ? Dungulph.

Usher Esq$^r$, son & heir of the said S$^r$ William Usher, in
S$^t$ Audeons Church, the said S$^r$ James weyms and Judith his
wife died without Issue Male, but had two daughters (viz$^t$) the
first mentioned Elizabeth and mary weyms, that died young.
The truth of y$^e$ premises is testified by the subscription of y$^e$
sd Xpher Usher Esq$^r$ Unkle to the defunct who returned this
Certificate to be recorded in the office of S$^r$ Richard Carney.

Page 527.   **Walter Kelly** of Goran son & heire of James Kelly of the
(814)   said towne departed this mortall life at Bristow in England
and was interred in the same town, he took to wife margreat
daughter of John Sayme by whom he had issue three daughters, margreat, sissily, & Joan. The truth of the premises is
testified by the subscription of margreat the relict of y$^e$ sd
Walter, who have returned this certificatt to be recorded in
the office vlster King of Arms, taken the 16 day of September
1635

MARGREAT KELLY        her mark

(815)   **Boetius M$^{cc}$ Egan** of Lisnekyragh in the County of
Galway Gent deceased, eldest son & heire of Connor m$^{cc}$ Egan
of y$^e$ same, Gent, eldest son & heir of Connor $^{mcc}$ Egan of y$^e$
same Gent, eldest son & heir of William m$^{cc}$ Egan of y$^e$ same
Gent, eldest son & heire of Teige m$^{cc}$ Egan of y$^e$ same Gent,
eldest son & heire of Boetius fynn m$^{cc}$ Egan of y$^e$ same Gent,
eldest son & heire of Boetius vir m$^{cc}$ Egan which boetius
descended

The said first menconed Boetius tooke to wife Margreat
daughter of Samuell m$^{cc}$ Egan, by whome he hath issue
2 sones & 1 daughter, (viz$^t$) Rorie eldest son & heire, who
tooke to wife Honora daughter of Richard m$^{cc}$ Enery of
Lurgan in the County of Mayo Gent.; Feagh m$^{cc}$ Egan 2$^d$ son
died young & unmarried; Mary m$^{cc}$ Egan only daughter
married to Donnagh m$^{cc}$ Egan of Creggan in the s$^d$ County of
Galway Gent. The said first Boetius departed this mortall
life at Lisnekeragh aforsaid the        of october 1634,
& was interred in y$^e$ Parish Church of Kilernane in the said
County. The truth of y$^e$ premises is testified by y$^e$ subscription of Rory m$^{cc}$ Egan eldest son of y$^e$ defunct, who hath
returned this Certificate to be recorded in my office  Taken
by me Thomas Preston Esq$^r$ Vlster King of Arms the 1$^{st}$ of
September (1639)        RORY M$^{cc}$ EGAN

(816)   **Teige O Dayly** of Dalyestowne in the County of Westmeath Gent, youngest son of Gullynaneoff, his son of 2$^d$
brother, who was married to Rose daughter of Teige O'Dally
of Dallystowne in the County of Cavan Gent, by whom he had

issue one son & 3 daughters, Donogh O Daly 3ᵈ brother maried to margreat daughter of John Tirrell of new Castle in the Com̃ of West meath Gent, by whome he had issue one daughter; Cochonach O Daly 4ᵗʰ brother maried to Gennett daughter of John Tuyte of Balrath in the said Com̃. of westmeath Gent, all which 4 brethren to yᵉ Defunct died without issue male. The first menconed Gullanneoff descended of the sept of owen O'neale. The said first menconed Teige O Daly Tooke to wife Ellinor daughter of Hugh mᶜᶜ Geoghegan of Killellyn in yᵉ said County of Westmeath Gent, by whom he had issue 9 sons & 4 daughters (vizᵗ) Cochonacht O'Daly eldest son maried Ellinor daughter of Teige O'Higgan of Kilbegg in the said Com̃ of Westmeath gent; Thomas 2ᵈ son as yett unmaried; Loughlin 3ᵈ son maried to mary daughter of Edward Nugent of Portlemane in yᵉ said Com̃ West meath Gent; Brian O Daly 4ᵗʰ son not maried; Richard 5ᵗʰ son; William 6ᵗʰ son; Teige 7ᵗʰ son; Farrell 8ᵗʰ son; & Neale the 9ᵗʰ son, five of yᵉ last died unmaried; Dorothy eldest daughter unmaried; Ellinor 2ᵈ daughter, meatre 3ᵈ daughter, & Dorothy 4ᵗʰ daughter, all unmaried.

The first menconed Teige O'Daly departed this life at Dallystowne aforesaid about yᵉ 20 of August 1633 and was intered in the Abby of Mollingar in the said County of Westmeath.

The truth of yᵉ premises is testified by the subscription of Cuchonacht O Daly eldest son yᵉ 18 of November 1637.

Cochonnaght O Daly.

**Walter Blake fitz Marcus** deceased the 5ᵗʰ of June *from* 1633 he had to wife mary Kirrowane the daughter of Peirce *Page 534.* Kirrowane of Gallway Gent, by whom he had issue one son *(817)* and 2 Daughters, Marius Blake, Jennit Blake & mary Blake; he was interred in the Abby of Sᵗ Francis in the County of          yᵉ premises above written are testified and signed by Clement Kirrowane brother-in-law to above, & was taken by Sʳ George Pary the last of August 1635.

---

This finishes the Funeral Entries.

---

[An Index of Surnames will be given in the future numbers of the JOURNAL.]

Lightning Source UK Ltd.
Milton Keynes UK
UKHW010859231118
332790UK00007B/374/P